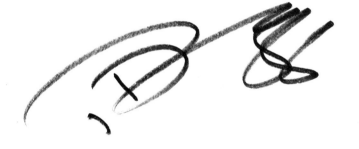

To
Billy Anne

UNDER
THE
INFLUENCE

UNDER
THE
INFLUENCE

BY **DR. PETER LEGGE**, OBC

WITH **TASHON ZIARA**

EAGLET PUBLISHING

Eaglet Publishing

Peter Legge Management Co. Ltd.
230 – 4321 Still Creek Drive
Burnaby, British Columbia, V5C 6S7 Canada
Tel. (604) 299-7311 Fax (604) 299-9188

Library and Archives Canada Cataloguing in Publication

Title: Under the Influence: How Influence Shapes the Person
    You Become / by Dr. Peter Legge, OBC, bestselling author
    of The Power of Tenacity.
Names: Legge, Peter, 1942- author.
Identifiers: Canadiana 20190170085 | ISBN 9780987819482
    (hardcover)
Subjects: LCSH: Influence (Psychology) | LCSH: Persuasion
    (Psychology) | LCSH: Interpersonal relations
Classification: LCC BF774 .L45 2020 | DDC 158.2—dc23

Jacket design by Rick Thibert; typeset by Ina Bowerbank;
edited by Matt Currie; cover jacket photograph and page 273
of Peter Legge by Ron Sangha

Printed and bound in Canada by Friesens Corporation

Dedication

To my wife of over 50 years,
Kay,
the gentle ways you continue to influence me
in all I do has been immense.
Thank you, I love you.

To my three daughters,
Samantha, Rebecca and Amanda,
God entrusted me with you,
and your influence on me has been considerable.

And to my seven grandchildren,
Benjamin, Cate, Carys, Grayson, London, Sophie and Oscar,
will I see your 21st birthdays? Maybe not.
Nevertheless, I will always love you.

UNDER THE INFLUENCE

INTRODUCTION

*"Setting an example is not the
main means of influencing others,
it is the only means."*
– Albert Einstein

On my 75th birthday, my three girls, Samantha, Rebecca and Amanda along with their husbands, took my wife Kay and me for an elaborate dinner at one of Vancouver's most prestigious restaurants: Bacchus, located in the Wedgewood Hotel.

Surrounded by the most important people in my life, I was exactly where I wanted to be, so the dinner could have been anywhere (but I'm not complaining; I love good food).

A round table for eight was perfect and we shared many stories and laughs together as we recounted some of the highs and lows over the years, including some of my embarrassing and unfortunate business mistakes and failures. With the whole family together, the evening was all about having fun and for me there is nothing greater or more important than that.

As I read the special wishes in my birthday cards, I was touched by my family's kind, loving words – which I felt undeserving of; for in my mind I often wondered if I really had done a good enough job as a father and husband to influence my precious family in a positive way to the best of my ability.

John Addison's quote from his book *Real Leadership* tells us, "People don't follow what you say. They follow what you do and who you are."

Leadership guru John Maxwell once said, "Leadership is about influence."

So, had I measured up? Together, my wife and I wondered: had we been good enough parents at influencing our three daughters in the right direction?

Kay had chosen to be a "stay-at-home" mom for their early, impressionable years, but as the girls grew older and became teenagers, they naturally grew independent. So Kay decided it was time to pursue her dream of becoming a professional counsellor. To do this, she had to go back to school to earn an undergraduate degree, which would enable her to then get her master's degree.

She enrolled in the Fraser Valley's Trinity Western University for both degrees, however, the night before she was to head off to campus for her first class she began to worry about her age.

She was 44 years old at the time and she said to me, "It's going to take me six years to complete my programs and by then I'll be 50 years old – who's going to hire me? I'll be too old."

I replied: "You're going to be 50 in six years anyway, so why worry about it, just go for it!"

She did, and six years later all of us were very proud as we watched her walk across the stage to receive her master's of counselling degree.

It took a long six years of commitment to study hard, attend classes, write lengthy research papers and complete homework assignments (which often meant sacrificing time with family). But our girls saw one determined and committed wife and mother earn almost straight "A's" during her six years of study. In fact, she only received a "C" in one class and that was because I had to have a serious cancer operation and needed more of her time and attention (which she gave, without hesitation).

All three of our daughters achieved university degrees, which they knew growing up was an expectation we had of them. But more important both to Kay and to me is the quality of their character; they are hard workers and all three of them are kind, thoughtful, polite, fun and good-natured.

Over the years, Kay and I have had an influence on our three beautiful daughters and now hopefully, we will have an opportunity to do the same with our seven wonderful grandchildren as they grow.

For each one of us, our influence must first be in the home.

And while Kay and I know we are far from perfect parents, we are both so proud of our daughters and their husbands.

In our desire to influence others in a significant way for their benefit, we might wonder at times, who really is watching? You might be surprised by the answer.

The average person directly or indirectly influences 10,000 other people during their lifetime and those in a position of leadership influence many, many more.

"Think before you speak. Your words
and influence will plant the seed of either success
or failure in the mind of another."
– Napoleon Hill

You might be surprised who is watching and being influenced by the example you set:

Your spouse
Your children
Your grandchildren
Your staff
Your customers
Your neighbours
Your friends
Your community

Now that we are more aware of all the people we have an opportunity to influence, let us be determined to be a good and positive influence.

Remember: your reputation enters the room before you do.

CHAPTER 1

LIFE IS A JOURNEY

"Always remember that adversity is not a detour,
it is part of the path. You will encounter obstacles. You will
make mistakes. Be grateful for both. Your obstacles
and mistakes will be your greatest teachers. And the only way
to not make mistakes in this life is to do nothing,
which is the biggest mistake of all."
– Richard Paul Evans

Although it's true that we are all living together on this wonderful planet we call home, each of us has our own path to take.

Since I was a small boy, I have been accustomed to travelling and taking on new journeys. I embarked on my first significant journey just five days before my fifth birthday, when my parents sent me away to Tavistock Hall Preparatory School (you can read all about it in the next chapter). As proper English parents, my mom and dad believed that it was important for me to have the right kind of influences in my life. As I stepped off the train and into a life of rules, order and discipline, my world was forever transformed.

Seven years later, my entire world changed once more when my parents decided to immigrate to Canada and we headed off together on a new adventure. I was 12 years old when our small family of three arrived in New Westminster and I quickly took on the moniker of "the English boy" at Vincent Massey Junior High School. I finished my secondary schooling at Lester Pearson High School (now called New Westminster Secondary) and the experiences and influences I encountered at both institutions had a significant impact on me during my formative years.

I'm not sure if it was just part of my nature or a learned behaviour, but even from a young age I endeavoured to make the most of my journeys and take in everything that was available to me. I also enjoyed sharing stories of my adventures, no matter if they were big or small.

Naturally, over the years, those stories have been a significant part of more than 5,000 speeches I've given and more than 20 books I have authored. What I've learned from sharing my experiences is that people love to hear stories; it really is a primal part of how we connect with one another and create community. It is also how we learn and develop as individuals.

Not all of our stories will have a happy ending. That's life!

Some will be stories of failure, loss, grief, rejection and despair, but these too have great value because they are the ones that make us stronger, teach us how to love and help us become wiser. They prepare us for the challenges that lead to a bigger and better story yet to come.

This book is filled with stories collected during the first 76 years of my journey. Stories of my experiences, both happy and sad; relationships that have grown; roads travelled; risks taken; aspirations achieved; problems conquered; rejections, recognitions, successes and failures . . . all of which I believe have made me better as a human being. The best part about the stories of my life is, good or bad, they are like old friends and I enjoy their company immensely.

> I believe we all have the seeds of greatness within us, but those seeds can only grow if we nurture them.

I believe we all have the seeds of greatness within us, but those seeds can only grow if we nurture them.

When former first lady of the United States Michelle Obama gave two presentations in Vancouver in 2018, one of the primary topics of conversation was who we *allow* to influence us.

"You decide what you let into your life," she told the audience, which included hundreds of young women who had received free tickets to the event courtesy of Vancity Credit Union. "One of the lessons that I grew up with was to always stay true to yourself and never let what somebody else says distract you from your goals."

It's easy to let ourselves be influenced by other people's expectations of how we should be living and easier still to be trapped by our own need for approval. But living your life according to someone else's expectations, making important decisions based on what others want rather than your own dreams or doing what is expected because you don't want to disappoint someone else, is a sure recipe for unhappiness. You can't live someone else's life, and sacrificing your own dream to please someone else simply leaves you exhausted and resentful. It takes courage to follow your own path in life and sometimes it can be a lonely journey, but there is also so much joy to be had along the way – that I promise you. It's worth the effort to ensure your own dreams and aspirations are the biggest influence in your life!

CHAPTER 2

WHAT MAKES YOU TICK?

D o you know what brings purpose and meaning to your life? How did you become the person you are today? What influences have you invited into your life? How will those influences shape the person you become tomorrow? Are you consciously deciding how you live your life?

One of the most recent books I've read is *Paul: A Biography* by Nicholas Thomas Wright (the former bishop of Durham in the Church of England and one of the world's leading New Testament bible scholars); the book is a biography of St. Paul the Apostle.

You may have heard someone call something in their life a "road to Damascus" experience, which refers to a sudden turning point in one's life. The term is in reference to St. Paul's conversion to Christianity while he was travelling along the road from Jerusalem to Damascus. Prior to that moment, he had been a Pharisee who persecuted followers of Jesus. A "road to Damascus moment" is a sudden transformation in personal belief or character which might be religious in nature, or it might not.

Almost every one of us at one time or another has our own "Damascus Road" experience.

Maybe as the result of a tragedy . . .

Maybe because of a bad habit that causes us to finally decide, "I can't live like this anymore . . ."

Maybe it was a breakup or divorce . . .

Maybe it was an accident . . .

Maybe, like Paul, you "encountered" God for the first time . . .

There are eight million stories in the naked city.

What's most important is what we learn from our experiences and how it changes our lives.

My mentor of over 50 years is Joe Segal. He's taught me a great deal about consciously choosing how to spend my time. He has also encouraged me to be very discriminating about what (and whom) I allow to influence my life. In fact, I wrote a whole book about it called *The Runway of Life*.

> What's most important is what we learn from our experiences and how it changes our lives.

Over the years, I have turned to Joe for guidance and advice on matters of both a business and personal nature. And while I struggled with my first company, I watched Joe build a veritable empire.

From humble beginnings with one store in 1950, he built a corporate chain of 70 Fields stores. In 1976, the year I started Canada Wide Media, Joe's corporation acquired Zellers and eventually became a large shareholder of the Hudson's Bay Company. After selling his retail empire, Joe went on to build a real estate empire with Kingswood Capital.

As the years turned into decades, our visits became a habit that I think both Joe and I enjoyed. Often they have taken place over lunch at Yew restaurant (formerly known as Chartwell) in the Four Seasons Hotel in downtown Vancouver, where Joe is such a fixture that he has his own table.

During many of our lunches, when there wasn't a particular issue at hand, I enjoyed sitting back and listening to Joe talk about his life and the lessons that experience has taught him. It was over one of these lunches, while Joe was expanding on his philosophy of life, that I got the idea for a book.

"Many people think of life as a road or a highway," Joe told me that day. "And that may be true in so much as there are many unexpected twists and turns and sometimes you get lost or end up at a destination that wasn't on the map. But if you think about it, a highway can go on forever, and life isn't like that. Life is more like a runway – because at some point you're going to run out of asphalt."

At this point, Joe picked up a napkin off the table and drew a horizontal line across it. At the beginning of the line he put a zero and at the end of the line he put the number 90. "That's how old I expect to be when I meet my maker," he said. Next, Joe wrote his current age on the line and turned to me. "The part of the line between zero and your current age, that's history, it's done, so forget about it."

Then he pointed to the section of the line between his current age and where he expects his runway to end. "The distance between where I am now and the end of my runway, that's all I've got to work with. So I have to ask myself, 'What am I going to do with the time that I have?' and whatever my answer is to that question, that's what I need to stay focused on."

I looked down at the napkin in Joe's hand and saw how short that section of the line was, then I thought about my own runway and started to break it down. If I'm fortunate enough to live to 90 years, that means just 25 more birthdays, 25 Christmas dinners with my family and 25 more glorious summers.

I realized in that moment that Joe was right, no matter what we have accomplished in the past – or how successful we have been–what really matters is the time we have ahead of us and what we choose to do with what's left of our runway. In that one simple yet powerful illustration, Joe had summed it up, and I told him right then, "This is a compelling idea and it would make a great book."

It has also become one of the key messages in my speaking engagements where I start out by drawing the runway on a piece of paper or a white board and filling in some numbers. Then, reminding my audience that all of our runways come to an end – sometimes with little or no warning – I ask them, "How much time are you willing to waste?"

While it can be frightening to consider how little time you have left on your own runway of life, it can also be motivating. We need to remember that although we can't slow down time, we can take control of how we use it.

The Runway of Life was inspired by Joe Segal, who is still going strong at 94 years of age. Joe is an original. Perhaps that is due in part to losing his father at a young age, or maybe it was something in the water in that small town of Vegreville, Alberta, where he grew up. Whatever the reason, Joe made a decision early in life to use only what works for him, to build an extraordinary life and to set an example that others could follow.

I've heard it said that great companies are not built by individuals who rely on somebody else to take care of them. They are built by men and women who rely on themselves, who dare to shape their own lives, who have enough courage to blaze new trails; individuals with enough confidence in themselves to take the necessary risks. When Joe left Vegreville as a young man to come to Vancouver, friends said, "It's so big you can't succeed." Joe said, "It's so big I can't miss."

Joe has often said to me that one of life's problems is not that we aim too high and fail. It is that we aim too low and succeed. No one could ever accuse Joe of aiming too low; he is an inspiration to me and everyone else who has had the good fortune to benefit from his generosity of spirit and his wisdom.

"If I can do it, anyone can do it," he often tells me.

It is up to each of us to decide what we will do with the time that we have. Hopefully, as you read through these pages, the stories and ideas presented within will resonate with you and help to illuminate your own unique path along the runway of life.

CHAPTER 3

BERNIE

"The fishermen know that the sea is dangerous
and the storm terrible, but they have never found these dangers
sufficient reason for staying ashore."
– Vincent Van Gogh

My father, Bernard Lawrence Legge, was born in Herfordshire, England. Shortly after he was born, the family moved to Barry, South Wales, which is about seven miles from the capital, Cardiff. Bernie, as he was called, was one of nine children in a family with limited resources; my grandfather was a railway porter for British Rail and my grandmother was a scullery maid.

When my grandmother first met my grandfather, his last name was spelled "Legg." My grandmother Edith didn't think it looked finished so she arbitrarily added an "e" to the end.

With such a large family, my grandparents struggled to put food on the table. Due to its proximity to the capital, Barry was a great shipping port and during his years at Cadoxton Primary School, my father often spent his free time watching the ships go in and out carrying every kind of cargo imaginable.

When he was 16 years old, seeing very little in the way of prospects for himself in Wales, my father came home from school and announced to his mother, "I am going to run away to sea!"

"Have a good time!" was her reply.

Bernie quickly procured a job as a cabin boy and the first ship he sailed on was called *Vancouver City*. It was named after the British explorer Captain George Vancouver and owned by the Smith Shipping Line. It was a 9,000-tonne freighter that transported iron ore. While he circumnavigated the globe many times, Bernie visited exotic locales on all five continents. He also visited Vancouver, British Columbia, six or seven times during his travels, a city that would one day play a significant role in the life of the Legge family (but I don't want to get ahead of myself).

When he finished his merchant marine career, Bernie settled in London and teamed up with some close friends to start a company called RLR Plastics, which was located on Wembley Way in London (within sight of Wembley Stadium, site of the 1948 Summer Olympics).

My father met my mother at a dance at the Hammersmith Palais in London, England (they were both fabulous ballroom dancers). He often told me that after the first time he saw her dance, he knew she was the best of the lot. She was also strikingly beautiful. They were such a graceful pair that even well into their 70s, when they would get up on the dance floor, people would clear the way just to watch them.

I never did find out how my father wooed my mother or how he proposed, but my parents married in Greenford, Middlesex, in 1937 and moved into a flat located at #7 Brookfield Court. I was born a few short years later on a cold blustery January day in 1942.

World War II was still going on at this time and my parents were concerned that the bombing of London might continue, so for safety reasons they bundled me off to Barry, South Wales, to be cared for by two of my favourite aunts, Auntie Bette and Auntie Bun. The purpose of sharing this story is to give you some idea of my deep, enduring connection with Wales. My only immediate cousins still live in South Wales, so a trip to the old country always includes a visit to Cardiff to see them, reconnect and share stories. In fact, one of my cousin's daughters now works with us here at Canada Wide Media.

When my grandmother first met my grandfather, his last name was spelled "Legg." My grandmother Edith didn't think it looked finished so she arbitrarily added an "e" to the end.

CHAPTER 4

TAVISTOCK HALL

Six days before my fifth birthday in early January 1947, my parents decided to enroll me into a boarding school – Tavistock Hall Preparatory School in Heathfield, Sussex. The train ride from Victoria Station to Heathfield was about 90 minutes. At the all-boys school, we were required to wear our uniform right from the beginning of the term, starting at Platform 6 of Victoria Station, where several teachers met us to take the train to school.

Following a tearful goodbye to my parents, the tone of the teachers seemed to change as the train pulled out of the station. Harsh discipline became the order of the day almost immediately. The first term was four months long – no parents, just 200 boys ranging from four to 11 years old.

My first kindergarten report card came in the summer of 1947. J.R. Ward, the headmaster of the school, wrote: "He can and

does do good work when he tries." Here's a copy, if you'd like
to see for yourself:

I'm not sure to what extent that comment made an impact on
me – I was just five years old.

Who really knows at such an early age how those years away from home, scared and lonely, came to shape me? They say we can be influenced without really knowing exactly where it comes from. I was just an ordinary little guy struggling to get along – to be average and accepted.

I found myself utterly alone and cried myself to sleep almost every night for at least four months. I think I thought it was just a nightmare and when I woke up I'd be back home in my own bed at Brookfield Court with my parents.

It's been said that our success or failure in life is not based on the good times but on how we deal with the bad times.

I honestly don't know how I managed to get through those first years at boarding school; I suspect that the love and admiration I had for my parents and my strong desire for their approval may have buoyed my resolve to maintain a brave face and tough it out.

> It's been said that our success or failure in life is not based on the good times but on how we deal with the bad times.

My father always taught me, "Never accept success or failure, since neither need be permanent."

While I wouldn't wish the experience of boarding school at the age of five on anyone and I wholeheartedly believe that my parents made this decision with the very best of intentions for the future success of their only child, I can also say that it instilled in me a strong sense of determination and I came to believe that in time, and with the right influence, I could move mountains.

Later, as I embarked on my career, I learned that we become like the people we spend time with, so I made a point of seeking out people that I admired to emulate. I never again wanted to be just average, not as a husband or father, not as a business leader, a speaker or as a Christian, and most certainly not as a grandfather.

CHAPTER 5

LIVING IN GREENFORD

I was reasonably oblivious to World War II, even though my father was in the London Fire Brigade stationed in Greenford and on-call 24/7.

He would often run down the back stairs, kitchen knife in hand, telling me he was going to cut Hitler's tail off.

It was a tough time, with food in short supply and ration books. Everyone was on edge expecting some devastating news as the bombing of London continued, but the three of us (mom, dad and me) were always happy.

As I mentioned earlier, my parents decided to send me to a private school for boys in East Sussex. The school was in a little town called Heathfield, halfway between what is now Royal Tunbridge Wells to the north and the seaside town of Brighton to the south.

I was enrolled at a private school because my parents felt it would afford me more opportunities than if I were to attend a regular school in London.

It was a big and brave decision for my mother and father. Both were working and the fees they'd have to pay would mean huge sacrifices. But it was one of the first big dreams they had for me. I would begin the next stage of my life with quality education, coupled with the kind of discipline that is traditionally part and parcel for the highly regulated private school system.

When the train left London's Victoria Station in the winter of the 1947, I was just five years old and we were puffing southward into the first big adventure of my young life. I had absolutely no idea what lay before me at Tavistock Hall Preparatory School for Boys in tiny Heathfield.

Uniforms were pretty standard at schools in post-war England, and even today they

> I urge you to be there at the starting line for your race, to give it your best every step of the way and to savour sweet victory when the race is done.

haven't changed much. We wore short grey pants, knee socks, a grey shirt, striped tie, a maroon blazer and a maroon cap, complete with the school crest.

With me on the train that morning were other London kids headed to the same destination. We sat together for the 90-minute journey and, at the tender age of five, that train trip could well have been a journey halfway around the world.

When I was 12, my parents decided that Canada, and specifically Vancouver, British Columbia, presented infinitely more opportunities for success than did post-war Britain. They were big dreamers and naturally my future was a big part of that.

The summer before we left for Canada was my last opportunity to participate in the annual Tavistock Sports Day. Full of vim, vinegar and Olympian dreams, I tried out for every event on the card, but the one in which I really wanted to excel was the Half Mile for Boys. At four times around the track, it was the glamour event, the premier race of the day. The winner invariably ended up being a school hero with adulation of the highest order and at least 15 minutes of fame.

After the time trials, they had a field of 15 – and sadly, I had not made the cut. I was disappointed, but what the heck, there were other events and I would still have the chance to depart from Tavistock Hall in style. But fate had other plans for me.

One of the traditions at Tavistock was for parents to donate trophies for specific Sports Day events. My parents had sent a trophy for, you guessed it, the Half Mile for 12-year-olds and, as you already know, at this stage I wasn't in the race!

Enter the headmaster.

There were 250 of us seated for breakfast when he arrived to deliver the news. As always happened when the "head" arrived, the hubbub within the dining room ceased in an instant. Not a whisper above the sea of porridge bowls.

He fixed me with a stare.

"Legge," he said. "You were too slow to be one of the runners in the Half Mile, but your parents have donated a trophy, so I guess I'll have to put you in the race."

It was incredible motivation for a 12-year-old boy!

When Sports Day arrived, there I was at the starting line, the 16th runner in a newly expanded field. The gun went off and we ran.

At the end of the first lap, I was dead last, exactly where I should have been. Then, as I passed the clubhouse turn, I caught the eyes of my mother, father and grandmother and knew that being last in the 1954 Legge Classic would not be good enough for the kid who bore the proud Legge name.

I put my butt in gear (or whatever the English equivalent of the expression might have been). Bigger steps, faster steps. Seeing my family had offered the injection of adrenaline I needed to really get going.

At the end of the second lap, I was in 10th place and my family were on the edge of their seats, cheering me on. At the end of the third lap, I was running fifth and victory seemed entirely possible. Team Legge was standing and cheering wildly.

In the final lap, the field dropped away behind me as I plunged victorious into the tape.

Against all odds, I won the race.

How did I win on that glorious day all those years ago? I don't exactly know, but I think that encouragement counted for a lot and, somewhere along the way, self-confidence kicked in as I strove for an attainable goal. Even the headmaster, in his strange way, had helped me along by throwing out the challenge in such a public fashion. I would show him that No. 16 could be No. 1.

I still have the little trophy my mother presented to me on that very special day.

Races aren't always exhausting physical endeavours. They can be as simple as setting a goal that you think may be just beyond reach, and then going for it. You'd be surprised how many times you can take home the prize, whatever it might be.

I have dreamed many dreams since that day at Tavistock Hall. Some of my dreams – many of them, in fact – have come true and what I have learned along the way is that most races are won lap by solid lap.

I urge you to be there at the starting line for your race, to give it your best every step of the way and to savour sweet victory when the race is done.

You won't win every race, but you can't win any race if you are not a participant.

CHAPTER 6

OH CANADA

"We all want to break our orbits, float like a
satellite gone wild in space, run the risk of disintegration.
We all want to take our lives in our own hands and
hurl them out among the stars."
– David Bottoms

E ven though the war ended in 1945, the whole country continued to suffer from the devastation and my parents decided that their future was not to be in England.

They spent many hours discussing where they should go, and in the end, the one place my father loved the most was Canada. They chose Vancouver, British Columbia, as our new home, and it was decided my father would travel ahead of us. "I'll go there for a year or so to get established and then I'll send for you and Peter," he told my mother.

Having landed on the East Coast, my father journeyed by train from Halifax to B.C. and got off at the last stop: New Westminster, where he found his first lodging at the YMCA on Royal Avenue. Eager to find a foothold in this new country, he tried his hand at just about everything, including picking blueberries and working as a short order cook at a café on Kingsway in Vancouver. He did whatever he could to earn money, but try as he might, no permanent opportunities came his way.

Lonely and discouraged, a year after arriving in the province, my father came to the conclusion that perhaps Canada was not the place for us after all. So he accepted a six-month contract working at a smelter in the northern community of Kitimat hoping to earn enough money to go back to England. However, just a few days before he was to head north, he heard about a job at a company called Gilley Brothers, which was located on the waterfront in New Westminster. He applied to become an inside sales rep selling concrete and other building supplies, and amazingly he got the job. So Kitimat never happened and he was able to realize his dream of bringing us to Canada.

The position at Gilley Brothers was a godsend for my father, but it was by no means easy for him. He often mentioned to me later on that in his early years at the company he was very much an outsider.

Bernie Legge ended up working at Gilley Brothers for 25 years, until he turned 65. In those days they had mandatory retirement and so when the day came, they thanked him for his service, threw him a party and wished him well.

Thankfully, my father wasn't quite ready to rest on his laurels just yet. When he first retired, I had just purchased *TV Week* magazine, so he decided to come work with me to negotiate the placement of our magazine racks in retail stores across the Lower Mainland. He was responsible for most of our *TV Weeks* being racked in prime locations, right at the checkout counters. Competing with the mighty *TV Guide* was always a challenge; when you're No. 2 in the market, you have to be nimble and creative to survive. With my dad's help, we were.

Flash-forward to a few years ago: we purchased *TV Guide*'s Vancouver and Victoria subscriber base, and today are the only paid television listings magazine in those markets.

> Competing with the mighty *TV Guide* was always a challenge; when you're No. 2 in the market, you have to be nimble and creative to survive.

We thought Bernie's job would take three or four months, but he ended up staying with the company for 20 years.

CHAPTER 7

THE INFLUENCE OF STRANGERS

"No true spiritual life is possible without a
generous heart. Generosity allies itself with an inner feeling
of abundance – the feeling that we have enough to share."
– Sharon Salzberg

My First British Passport #D919A58 admitted me as a landed immigrant to Canada at the Pacific Highway Crossing on March 30, 1954. I was just 12 years old. It was the beginning of my Canadian adventure.

My mother and I had sailed from Southampton to New York and after a couple of nights in the Big Apple, we took a Greyhound bus from New York across the United States through Chicago. Our last stop before arriving in New Westminster was Seattle, Washington.

My mother took me to the coffee shop in the Seattle

Greyhound depot for a short break before the three-hour ride to our final destination.

My mother didn't tell me that she was flat broke as I ordered my first hamburger, fries and Coke in North America (while she had a pot of tea). As a child, it didn't even occur to me that she might be concerned about how to pay for the meal. Thankfully, a kind lady sitting next to us seemed to sense that mom had no money and offered to pay – it was less than $5.

Throughout my life, I have often thought of that nameless woman and her generosity towards two people she had never met. Shortly after picking up our cheque, she quietly slid out of her seat and disappeared. As one of my very first encounters in this new world, it made a lasting impression on me – and I remember wondering, "Is that what they mean – to be kind to strangers?"

Very often it is not the size of the gift that matters, but the awareness that someone is in need and there's something you can do to help.

> Very often it is not the size of the gift that matters, but the awareness that someone is in need and there's something you can do to help.

That act of generosity was my first North American teaching point and I have never forgotten it.

The simplest gifts can indeed last a lifetime and I am sure this encounter has influenced me many times and encouraged me to be as generous as I can.

Over the years, I have been inspired to help numerous organizations raise millions and millions of dollars for very worthy causes. We've also scheduled millions of dollars worth of free ad pages in our various magazines for dozens of very worthy charities. And perhaps it all started with a hamburger, fries and Coke!

CHAPTER 8

PETER'S PLAGUE

"The world moves so fast these days
that the man who says it can't be done is generally
interrupted by someone doing it."
– Elbert Hubbard

My entire business life has been in or around media, and it all started with one flippant remark way back in Grade 12.

I was a student at New Westminster's Lester Pearson High School, named after Canada's 14th prime minister, considered to be one of the most influential Canadians of the 20th century.

I was taking an optional course called "English 32" – which taught students how to be writers. (Not a bad class to take in your final year of high school.) Our teacher was Frank Shepard, who also oversaw the production of the school newspaper, *The*

Mike. "Mike" was Lester Pearson's nickname and in addition to the school paper, all of our various sports teams were also named after him.

Mr. Shepard's journalism class was responsible for writing and producing six issues each school year. I had a regular column called "Peter's Plague," which was essentially a round-up of high school tidbits and name drops. All the kids clamoured to grab a paper to see if their name was mentioned!

At the time, one of the oldest daily newspapers in the province was *The Daily Columbian*, headquartered in New Westminster. Its publisher, Rikk Taylor, was a guest speaker at our class. He was a dynamic guy – positive and inspiring, he totally captivated us students with stories of putting out an award-winning paper six days a week.

Mr. Taylor spoke highly of his editors and dozens of reporters who prepared imaginative news stories with a focus on New West. Back then, the *Columbian* even rivalled the highly successful *Vancouver Sun* and *Province*.

At the end of Mr. Taylor's presentation, a cheeky kid named Peter Legge shot up his hand and asked, "Who makes the most money at your newspaper?"

The class laughed but they too were eager to know.

"Not the writers," Mr. Taylor answered, "but the salespeople!"

I retorted, "Well then, I don't want to be a writer, I want to be a sales guy!"

Mr. Taylor challenged me, "When you graduate in June, why

don't you come down and see me?"

You might be wondering if I went to the *Columbian*'s offices after school finished for the year. Well, I'm sorry to say the weather was simply too good and it was shaping up to be a fine summer, so I chose to enjoy my freedom from high school and wait until after Labour Day.

When that day finally came, I put on a smart shirt, a tie and a jacket and made sure my shoes were spotless. No doubt channelling my father Bernie's gumption, I marched on down to the *Columbian* HQ on Sixth Street, breezed into the reception and proudly announced that Mr. Rikk Taylor was expecting me. Talk about cheek!

> I marched on down to the *Columbian* HQ on Sixth Street, breezed into the reception and proudly announced that Mr. Rikk Taylor was expecting me. Talk about cheek!

Obviously, he had no idea who I was but he was gracious with his time and agreed to sit down. I reminded him of how we met and he hired me on the spot for $39 a week.

My first step into the media business had been taken.

CHAPTER 9

IF YOU COULD MAKE IT IN LONDON

*If the '50s were in black-and-white, then
the '60s were in Technicolor – the swinging '60s
remain the defining decade for Britain.*
– Historic U.K.

My days at Lester Pearson High School during the late '60s saw me serving as entertainment during most school assemblies, and I soon caught the showbiz bug as a standup comedian. Dozens of subsequent engagements in British Columbia whetted my appetite. But I had bigger dreams . . .

If you could make it in London in the swinging '60s, that was the place to be. It was glorious – a revolution that was every would-be entertainer's dream. On Carnaby Street with its artsy vibe and mod fashions, the city came alive with a new generation

– and a new sound. Leading the way were rock musicians like The Rolling Stones, The Yard Birds and Jimi Hendrix. The Animals with *House of the Rising Sun.* Tom Jones with those hips. Not to mention Lulu with her No. 1 hit single "To Sir With Love," Dionne Warwick with "Walk on By," The Kinks, Engelbert Humperdinck . . . and of course, The Beatles.

England even had its very first commercial radio station, broadcasting from a ship in the middle of the North Sea. Radio Caroline (or Pirate Radio, as it was dubbed) played rock music that couldn't be heard on the BBC and was the first station to sell commercial airtime to advertisers.

Around this time, the venerable London Hippodrome was renamed The Talk of the Town and featured appearances by many of the most popular international artists of the time including Diana Ross & the Supremes, Judy Garland, Eartha Kitt, The Temptations, Frank Sinatra, The Carpenters, Ella Fitzgerald, Liza Minnelli, The Jackson 5, Paul Anka, Stevie Wonder and Neil Sedaka.

The Talk of the Town was located smack in the middle of London's vaunted West End, just a stone's throw from Leicester Square; it was the place to see all of the really big names who always seemed to play BBC TV and ITV "A."

My future wife Kay and I had met on a voyage from Vancouver, through the Panama Canal and across the Atlantic to Lisbon, landing in Southampton in 1968 following a 27-day cruise. Kay was a passenger and I was one of the featured entertainers.

We were both headed to London. Kay was going to stay with her girlfriend Jill and I was going to a humble flat just off Brompton Road, a few blocks from the world-famous Harrods – still one of the world's greatest department stores.

After our time together on the ship, neither of us could stop thinking about the other. As she commuted each day to the West End to work in the fashion district, I started to play the nightclub circuit as a standup comic.

I was booked for two weeks in the Theatre Royal Stratford in a revue called *Girls Will Be Boys*. During that period it was all the rage and it was paid work, after which performers would often do evening gigs at different nightclubs.

Similar revues saw me appearing at the London Playboy Club on Pall Mall – the best cellar in the city – and a host of one-night appearances in an assortment of other clubs including George Raft's spot in Barkley Square.

Show business was brisk and when you threw in a few shipboard gigs from Southampton to the Canary Islands and a 16-day trip aboard the SS *Canberra*, I had a pretty good year all in all.

Not long after returning to London, Kay and I got married and moved into a small two-bedroom townhouse in East Putney – a short walk to the Underground tube station. It was an easy connection for Kay to the fashion district and easy access for me to the theatre district. It was a very productive time, but it wasn't moving fast enough for me.

The opportunity to perform on television eluded me. Nearly all of the evening television shows in the '60s were populated by well-established performers, who were in constant demand on both BBC and ITV. As such, it was virtually impossible for a new guy to break into British TV. I did a couple of bit parts on a hit police drama, playing Inspector Parsons on BBC's *Softly, Softly*. Unfortunately, my only speaking scene was left on the cutting-room floor by the time the 50-minute

> This was a once-in-a-lifetime opportunity and I wanted to make the most of it. I had three weeks to write the best 25-minute show I could think of.

episode was edited for time . . . so Inspector Parsons was left speechless! I still got paid, but it was a frustrating time.

The biggest ratings of the day were garnered by BBC's *Morecambe & Wise Show*, which featured two of the funniest entertainers of their generation. They were stars in every sense of the word and Britain's greatest double act. Ernie Wise and Eric Morecambe had been performing together since before I was born and they had even shared a stage at the Hippodrome with Billy Cotton, who was head of BBC night entertainment by the time I came on the scene. If I wanted to break into the TV business, he was the guy I had to reach . . . but how to do that?

Living next door to us in Putney's Lake Place were Peter and Carol Thiery. Peter was an independent television producer and Carol was a regular host on daytime TV.

As we got to know our neighbours, I decided to use the

opportunity to pitch an idea to Peter. I asked him if his producer boss would consider donating some time at the company's independent studio on a Friday afternoon. I would write a script, his wife Carol could host and Peter could produce the piece, which I could then use as my demo video to pitch a show to the big networks.

Peter took the idea to his manager, who said yes.

We would get the studio and staff for exactly 25 minutes on a Friday afternoon, between 4:35 and 5 p.m.; however, at 5 o'clock exactly, he would pull the plug and let everyone go home.

We agreed on a day and my creative juices started to flow. This was a once-in-a-lifetime opportunity and I wanted to make the most of it. I had three weeks to write the best 25-minute show I could think of.

As the day grew closer, we rehearsed the script I had developed and borrowed costumes and props from various sources; the crew and the studio staff were almost as excited as I was. The studio boss reminded me no less than seven times that we would have exactly 25 minutes to produce my demo.

Was I ready?

We would only have one opportunity to get it on tape.

We squeezed in a few more rehearsals, and then it was time; the lights came on, the cameras rolled and 25 minutes later the crew brought down the curtain, unplugged the equipment and headed home for the weekend. I thanked Peter for his help, and Kay and I went straight to the nearest pub in Fulham with our brand-new demo in hand.

As we sat across from one another and celebrated with a pint, we talked excitedly about making my big break into television and who needed to see the video in order for that to happen.

A couple of pints later, we had a plan.

We would rent a screening room in London and invite the top nighttime entertainment directors from BBC and ITV to an intimate cocktail party/screening. After some discussion, we targeted six high-level executives – all six said yes to the invite, including John Ammonds, producer of *Morecambe & Wise*. He was the key connection we were looking for.

The night arrives, and after a few light sandwiches and a couple glasses of wine, it was time for the show . . .

It was called *Don't Ask Us, We're New Here*, and we pitched it as a sketch comedy/variety program that would introduce new talent to British audiences. It would feature five new performers, including me as the host.

John Ammonds was reasonably impressed and invited me to join him on his cab ride back to the BBC Studio in Shepard Bush – a 50-minute trip. During those 50 minutes, we hammered out the details of the new show. John took the concept to the aforementioned BBC exec Billy Cotton and he loved it. A contract was drawn up and the show was given a nine-week run in primetime on Friday evenings from 7:55 to 8:20 p.m. I was paid £50 as a performer, £50 as a contributing writer and even £5 as the warm-up act before the show.

It was a dream come true.

The show had a short life, but garnered an audience of nine million viewers by the end of its run. I eventually abandoned my ambition of being a comedian . . . but it was an amazing ride while it lasted. I wouldn't have missed it for the world.

CHAPTER 10

THE NIGHT NOBODY LAUGHED

*"Give me six hours to chop down a tree
and I will spend the first four sharpening the axe."*
– Abraham Lincoln

We all make mistakes in life, a few turn out to be big mistakes, but most offer us an experience we can learn from and keep moving forward. They are indicators along the way to help us figure out what works, what doesn't and where we want to go next. Some mistakes even help us refine our character and grow.

I made such a mistake and it taught me something that has stayed with me ever since.

During my time in the U.K. as a comedian, I had some success making people laugh and figured that with a bit of British luck, I'd go straight to the top.

But in show business, there are always dues to pay and, worst of all, audiences to eat you alive!

Let this next tale be a lesson . . .

I landed a gig in Wales doing a circuit of 20 working men's clubs for £6 a night. The mission: try to get the blokes who had been toiling away down in the mine all day to enjoy a few laughs along with their beer.

I knew nothing about Wales. I couldn't pronounce the names of half the towns I was visiting (you try it!) and knew even less of the local happenings and current affairs. But that didn't seem too important; humour has universal appeal and I steered clear of any political commentary or stance.

One rainy night in a small Welsh village called Aberfan, it was my turn to go on, right after the singer and the magician. I stepped in front of the microphone and went right into my schtick about kids. I told over-the-top jokes about how rotten they can be, how ungrateful and unnecessary they really are. Real funny stuff that had audiences cracked up in London.

Not this time. Not a laugh – nor even a murmur of a laugh.

Twelve minutes later, exasperated at the lack of response, I gave up, walked off the stage and right into the angry face of the club owner.

"Alright, mate. On your way," he said and pointed to the back door. His mouth was clenched and his eyes livid, "Get outta town!"

Hurt at being given the bum's rush and puzzled by the lack

of response to what had been a proven routine in all the clubs before this one, I slunk back to the hotel.

"Aberfan . . . Aberfan . . ." I muttered to myself as I took note of the town's name on each storefront. "Aberfan."

Then it all came together and I knew exactly where I'd gone wrong. In 1966, on a hilltop high above the town's small primary school, a tip (i.e. the massive leftover pile from the diggings in a coal mine) had slipped and raced down the hillside. It slid like a great grey blanket over the school and took the lives of 170 people, most of them children. A catastrophic loss, it had been the worst disaster in Aberfan's history and the pain and shock were still very, very fresh in the minds of everyone who lived there.

> Never again will I step in front of a microphone without knowing my audience.

Many of the working men in the club that night were the fathers of those children – still utterly grief-stricken. I felt awful about my ignorance.

That experience still lives with me today and I will never forget the men who sat in front of me that night. It profoundly changed the way I prepare for each new client meeting or speaking gig. Never again will I step in front of a microphone without knowing my audience.

It is so important to know who you are addressing. If you don't, as I found out that night, you get exactly what you deserve.

What's more, just as you would do your homework before an interview or an important meeting, it also serves you well to learn the customs and culture before travelling to a new country. A few minutes of research can save your reputation, sometimes even your life.

CHAPTER 11

MAN WALKS ON THE MOON

*"For one priceless moment in the whole history
of man, all the people on this Earth are truly one."*
– President Richard Nixon, in a telephone call
to Neil Armstrong and Buzz Aldrin while they were
on the moon

It was an event that changed history. On a clear July evening, man walked on the moon! It was Wednesday, July 20, 1969, and Kay and I were living in a small townhouse at 1 Laker Place, Putney, England. Our front door was wide open and a giant crystal-clear moon beamed down on our tiny living room, filling the entire house with its light. We knew something big was about to happen.

I can remember saying to Kay as we watched David Frost host the lunar landing program on British television. "Katie, can you believe this? At this exact moment, two men are up there walking on the surface of the moon."

In our imagination, looking out the front door, we thought we could actually see them some 238,900 miles away.

The *Apollo 11* module touched down on the face of the moon at exactly 4:18 EDT.

The three-man crew for the moonshot was led by Neil Armstrong, who said, "Houston, *Tranquility Base* here. The *Eagle* has landed."

As Armstrong set foot on the surface, he uttered what has become one of the most famous quotes in modern history, "That's one small step for man, one giant leap for mankind."

Minutes later, the second man on the moon, Buzz Aldrin, chimed in. "I would like to request a few moments of silence, I would like to invite each person listening in, wherever and whomever he may be, to contemplate for a moment the events of the past few hours and to give thanks in his own individual way."

Then Aldrin reached for the wine and bread he'd brought to space – the first foods ever poured or eaten on the moon. "I poured the wine into the chalice our church had given me. In the one-sixth gravity of the moon, the wine curled slowly and gracefully up the side of the cup," he later wrote. Then, Aldrin read some scripture and ate. Armstrong looked on quietly but did not participate.

A one-in-a-billion goal had been achieved and I wondered

just how many men and women were part of that extraordinary mission and shared in what could only be described as a monumental achievement. NASA estimated that it had taken more than 400,000 engineers, scientists and technicians to accomplish the moon landings (a number that reflects the vast array of systems and subsystems needed to build everything and deploy the mission).

> The future might not hold a moon landing for you and me – but the realization of our dreams and the fulfillment of our goals is what life is made of.

What's more, many of the people involved had never worked in the aerospace industry, and none of them had ever worked on machines designed to transport humans to another world. Overnight, as their companies won Apollo contracts, their jobs suddenly took on a greater purpose.

According to a 50th-anniversary story in *The Guardian*, "The near-impossible task of managing this vast pyramid of people across America fell to the Apollo programme manager George Müller and, in a stroke of genius, he called upon the astronauts themselves for help; each national hero would make personal visits to the factories making all these parts. It was a crucial reminder to the workers that a single technical glitch could kill a man they had personally met. And it compelled each of them to devote their lives to Apollo for the best part of a decade."

The future might not hold a moon landing for you and me – but the realization of our dreams and the fulfillment of our goals is what life is made of.

"Shoot for the moon!" as the saying goes and you might miss it, but at least you'll be among the stars.

What stars do you want to reach?

CHAPTER 12

THE POWER OF "YES"

"If somebody offers you an amazing opportunity
but you are not sure you can do it, say yes –
then learn how to do it later!"
– Richard Branson

L et me share the power of saying, "Yes."

I've taken a lot of risks in my life and I must say the one I took when I said yes to going back to Vancouver while I was making the rounds as a standup comic in the U.K., was one for the books.

This yes led to more yeses, which established the foundation for the most productive and philanthropic years (or dare I say, decades) of my life.

The First Yes

I was working in London, doing shows in various nightclubs around the city as well as Birmingham, South Wales and Bristol; however, I was still represented by Vancouver show business leader Ben Kopelow. Ben called me and said that Ken Stoffer of the legendary Cave theatre and restaurant (on Hornby Street in Downtown Vancouver) was having The Mills Brothers perform in two weeks.

Whoa! The Mills Brothers had been superstars from the 1930s through to the 1950s. Their remarkable voices (which could mimic musical instruments) brought them to the peak of their chosen field and their records, like *Ole Rockin Chair*, *Lazy River*, *How I'm Doin'* and many others, sold millions of copies.

When Ben asked if I would return to Vancouver to be the opening act for the world-famous duo, I thought, "This is an opportunity not to be missed." In fact, fronting one of the best and smoothest vocal groups in the industry was a dream come true for me.

My answer to Ben's offer was a resounding, "Yes!"

The Second Yes

When I arrived in Vancouver, I realized I didn't have enough of a wardrobe for a two-week gig, and what I did have wasn't classy enough for the likes of the Cave.

I needed clothes but didn't have enough money to buy a new suit.

Luckily, I bumped into Murray Goldman, a clothier and

professional acquaintance of mine, on the street. After greeting one another and a few pleasantries, Murray said, "I hear you're opening for the Mills Brothers next week, how exciting!"

I shared my enthusiasm for the gig and then told him about my wardrobe issue and without missing a beat, he said, "No problem, come by my store at 166 Hastings Street tomorrow and we'll fit you out."

"Murray, I have no money," I said.

"You don't need any," he replied. "Suits, ties, socks, shoes, it's all on me. You need to look your best on stage; my wife and I will be ringside on opening night."

Wow! Wow! Wow! How could I refuse? I thanked Murray profusely and the next day when I showed up at his shop he proved good as his word. I was looking dapper for my big moment.

Murray and his wife came to a few shows during my engagement at the Cave and some might say my outfits were better than my jokes.

Murray Goldman went on to become one of Vancouver's most colourful (and successful) business leaders, who also co-founded Big Brothers of Greater Vancouver.

The Third Yes

The Mills Brothers did not disappoint. We had two sold-out

shows every night for two weeks. Vancouver loved them . . . and I enjoyed every minute of my time as the opening act.

During the second week, on a Wednesday, Peter and Jeffrey Barnett of Pizza Patio fame (and later Elephant & Castle Pubs) came to the Cave and somehow got backstage and cornered Harry Mills. Jeffrey suggested that after our closing show, they would send a limo to pick up the Mills Brothers and myself and take us to the Queen Elizabeth Theatre, where they were conducting a telethon for the new Variety Club charity.

"So what do you want from us?" asked Harry.

"You boys sing some of your hits and Peter, you can tell some jokes."

"Then what happens?" asked Harry.

"People phone in and donate money, which all goes to very needy children in Canada."

"I don't think so, that will never happen," said Harry. "Why would people phone in to give money?"

"That's what a telethon is, people watch the entertainment on TV and phone in to donate," the Barnetts told him.

Neither Harry Mills nor I had ever heard of anything like it.

"What do you think?" Harry asked, turning to me.

"Let's give it a try," I replied.

The limo picked us up after the show.

The Mills Brothers sang some songs.

I told some jokes.

The phones rang.

The telethon gathered millions of dollars in donations and I, for one, was hooked.

As of last February, when I co-emceed the 53rd-anniversary telethon at Vancouver's Hard Rock Casino, I have been performing and supporting Variety for 43 consecutive years. Since its inception, Variety has raised hundreds of millions for special-needs kids in British Columbia.

Veteran show business giant Danny Thomas once said, "Nobody stood so tall as he who stooped to help a child."

That's the power of yes!

CHAPTER 13

TURNING PEBBLES INTO DIAMONDS

"Opportunities are like sunrises,
if you wait too long you miss them."
– William Arthur Ward

Beginning in my 30s, I was a camp manager at Young Life's magnificent Camp Malibu, which is situated about 100 miles north of Vancouver in Princess Louisa Inlet. Part of my responsibility each summer was to prepare and deliver eight different talks a week for three weeks. My first message would always start with a story or parable that I hoped would inspire my teenaged audience to look for opportunities, even in the most difficult situations of their lives.

Here is one of my favourites from that time:

Many years ago, a young man found himself alone on

a rocky beach with his empty backpack. Walking along the shore, much to his surprise a genie appeared.

"Fill your backpack with as many pebbles as you can and when you open it in the morning, you will be both happy and sad," she told him.

Just as quickly as the genie had appeared, she was gone.

The young man did as he'd been instructed and after a pretty good night's sleep, he opened his backpack to see

When you're presented with an obstacle, step back for a moment and try to see how you can turn it to your advantage.

what was inside. To his delight, all of the rocks had turned to diamonds, which made him very happy indeed; although he was also sad that he had not picked up more pebbles.

What pebbles do you have in your backpack that could have been turned to diamonds?

The books you read, the people you meet, the questions you ask, the places you go and the career you choose.

The mistakes that you've made and learned from, the setbacks you've encountered and found your way around.

Your experiences can always turn pebbles into diamonds if you look for the opportunity that may be disguised as a problem. Below is a perfect example.

The Royal Palace in Tehran, Iran, contains what is undoubtedly one of the most beautiful mosaic masterpieces in the world. The interior walls and ceiling sparkle with multifaceted reflections as if encrusted with thousands upon thousands of diamonds. However, this vision of beauty is not quite as it was intended to be.

When the palace was first designed, the architect specified that huge sheets of mirrors should hang on the walls. Unfortunately, when the first shipment of mirrors arrived from Paris, the builders discovered that the glass had been shattered in transit. The contractor promptly threw the mirrors into the trash and informed the architect of the problem.

To the surprise of all, the architect did not despair at this news. Instead, he ordered that all of the broken pieces be gathered together and brought to him. The architect then proceeded to smash the glass into even smaller shards before ordering that they be glued to the walls, creating a mosaic of shimmering glass.

Obviously, the architect had the eye of an artist to be able to take something broken and turn it into a masterpiece. However, there is another lesson to be gleaned from the story and it is this: If we simply choose to see it from a different angle, what looks like an obstacle to success can in fact be a glorious opportunity.

Obstacles are a fact of life, we all encounter them. What's important is how we deal with them. When you're presented with an obstacle, step back for a moment and try to see how you can turn it to your advantage.

If you're looking for a job and feeling the frustration of not enough opportunity, here's something to consider: 80 per cent of jobs that come available never get advertised. Why? Because they end up being filled by a candidate who knew someone who knew the person doing the hiring. Many employers would rather take a chance on a person who is recommended to them than hire someone who has answered a job ad. So what is the pebble here? Work the network you already have; reach out to friends, family, neighbours, former employers and community contacts and let them know you're looking for a new opportunity. Next, expand your network; introduce yourself to new people, go to networking events, share on your social media channels (both personal and professional); volunteer or get involved with organizations related to the industry you're interested in.

Want to make a more impactful first impression when you arrive for the interview? Try this. Go to the office three days before your interview and introduce yourself to the person at the reception desk, let's call her Mary. Make a note of Mary's name for future reference and tell her that you are just checking that this is the right building, right floor, etc. for your meeting in a few days.

When you come back for your interview, greet Mary by name and after she escorts you to the office of the boss (or interviewer), make sure you say something like, "Nice to see you again, Mary," as she is leaving the room.

Chances are, the boss/interviewer will say something like, "You know each other?" to which you can simply nod. Just like that, you are no longer a stranger applying for a job and the perception of your connection changes the dynamic of the interview in your favour.

CHAPTER 14

IT ALL STARTED WITH A 10-CENT MAGAZINE

"It can be liberating to get fired because you realize the world doesn't end. There's other ways to make money, better opportunities."
– Ron Livingston

I've spent nearly my entire working life in media – radio, TV, print – and it has served me well. It's an ever-changing business that takes no prisoners and requires enormous stamina and creativity; to sustain success in this industry for 45 years is not for the faint of heart. I have also been blessed with a long career speaking and inspiring others to reach for their dreams. Whether it is in my office or at a speaking engagement, not a week goes by without someone asking me how I started *TV Week* magazine (which was my first foray into the publication business), what challenges I faced in those early years and how it became so successful.

Most beginnings aren't very sexy . . . or necessarily easy and my story is no different in that regard. It started with failure, which I suppose could have been viewed as a bad thing. But what if, as we talked about in the first chapter of this book, a failure such as losing your job presents you with the opportunity to follow a lifelong dream? What if it wakes you up to the fact that you really didn't like that job anyway? What if it helps you realize you were just marking time because you were scared to take a leap of faith and make a change?

What then?

I believe that most of us are far more afraid of failure than we need to be. Failure is a wonderful tool that acts like an alarm bell, helping us to realize when we need to make adjustments in our plan or ditch the plan altogether and make a new one. As long as we are willing to keep going and try new things, we aren't failing, we're learning.

In my own life, it took getting fired to finally motivate me to fulfill a longstanding dream to own my own business.

It was the summer of 1976 and Joe Chesney was an on-air personality at New Westminster's CKNW on Columbia Street. Joe and a group of investors applied to the national regulator for a radio licence to start a new country music station in the city of Langley. The call letters were to be CJJC. It was the only AM radio station in the Langley area at the time.

As the station became established in the market, Joe realized that he needed a competitive sales department to compete with the bigger stations in Vancouver for advertising dollars and he offered me the position of general sales manager.

I jumped at the opportunity and thought my media connections throughout the Lower Mainland would be an asset. Although Joe and I had certain philosophical differences, he was very encouraging of my sales approach and in pretty short order our ad revenue exceeded the station's budget. We were off and running.

As the station became more established, Joe pretty much left the sales department to me as he tended to his on-air duties in addition to running the business and building a community presence. However, as the station grew in prominence and profitability, the relationship between Joe and me did not.

On a Thursday morning just before noon – we never seem to forget the little details of significant turning points in our lives – a short memo went out to the staff that said: "Peter Legge is no longer employed by this station. It will be business as usual." Signed Joe Chesney.

Business as usual? Maybe for the station but certainly not for me!

It was the first time I'd ever been fired and I vowed right then that it would also be the last.

As with anyone who has ever been fired, I wondered why it happened. I thought I'd done a pretty good job handling the department, competing with the bigger Vancouver radio market, exceeding sales budgets every month and getting the station recognized far beyond our broadcast borders. For three years we had even scooped up the World Hockey Association broadcast rights and sold them out. I thought things were going pretty well. I'd even made a costly personal investment in the station. There is no question that the owner and I had differences and while I resented and strongly disagreed with his reasons for my termination, it *was* his station and he had every right to decide who would work for him and who wouldn't. Clearly I didn't fit into his plans.

It was a 45-minute drive from work to my house in Coquitlam where I would have to break the news to Kay. I had no idea how she would respond when I told her there would be no more commissions and no severance pay. I'm not a particularly fast driver and this was before cellphones, so I had a lot of time to think on my way home. When I arrived, I was a little nervous as I parked the car and prepared to face the music.

How would Kay react?

What would she say?

Would she get mad?

Would she blame me for not being a good provider?

Would she leave me?

My mind was racing.

I opened the back door and walked in.

"You're home early," Kay commented. "How did your day go?"

"Let's have a glass of wine and chat," I suggested.

As we sat down, Kay knew something was up.

"OK, what is it?" she asked.

"I got fired earlier today; I no longer have a job!" I confessed.

Holding my breath, I waited for a reaction, expecting her to be upset or angry.

"Good!" said Kay. "You shouldn't be working for someone else, anyway; you should be working for yourself. You're smart, you're creative and you're the best salesman in town; maybe it's time to get into your own business."

> My departure from that station was the catalyst for actions that set me on a course of daring and courageous decisions – some of the biggest I have ever made.

Wow! Talk about support. While I was still in shock, I hadn't considered that this might be a good thing. Over the next several days, Kay's words echoed through my mind.

Sometimes – actually, quite often – what seems like a disaster can change your life for the better. The power of words!

My departure from that station was the catalyst for actions that set me on a course of daring and courageous decisions – some of the biggest I have ever made. I had a wife and child to support but I was heavily in debt; my house was mortgaged to the hilt and I had cashed in all my life insurance to buy 10 per cent of the station . . . and now I was on the street with no notice, no golden handshake and no termination pay. Nothing.

The circumstances I found myself in reminded me of the

story of Julius Caesar crossing the Rubicon in 49 B.C. The Rubicon is a shallow river that, in Caesar's time, acted as a northern boundary of Italy. As the governor of a northern territory whose governorship was about to expire, the Roman Senate instructed Caesar to disband his army and return to Rome. Caesar was explicitly ordered not to march his soldiers across the Rubicon and into Rome; to do so would be an act of treason and a declaration of war against the Senate.

According to some historians, Caesar is said to have uttered the phrase *"Alea iacta est"* – "The die is cast" – as he led his army across the shallow river, thus beginning the Roman Civil War. Today, the phrase "Crossing the Rubicon" is a metaphor for making a fateful decision or passing the point of no return.

Despite the fact that I was behind the eight ball financially, I made my own decision to cross the Rubicon when I decided that I would never again work for someone else.

Former U.S. president Theodore Roosevelt once said, "Far and away the best prize that life has to offer is the chance to work hard at work worth doing."

It was high time that I started working for myself and building my own empire.

Timing, as they say, is everything. Enter Al Davidson.

"Big Al" was the most listened-to and quoted sports director in Greater Vancouver on the mighty 98 – CKNW. With a booming voice and strong opinions, everyone knew Big Al.

To say he was a bit bombastic is an understatement of the

highest magnitude, but boy did people like to tune in for his broadcasts and argue about his opinions. Having worked for a short time in the sales department of CKNW, I knew this firsthand.

When any of Big Al's daily broadcasts came up for sponsorship, selling them was like shooting ducks in a barrel; you couldn't miss. That's not to say that people were clamouring to sign up. Most often, when I made the sales call, the conversation went something like this:

Potential advertiser: "There's no way I'm going to buy an ad on Al Davidson's broadcast."

Me: "You don't have to love Al, but there's no one who gets people's attention quite the way he does. Before you decide, answer me this:

"Who's the sports director on CJOR?"

Don't know.

"Who's the sports director on CKLG?"

Don't know.

"Who's the sports director on CBC?"

Don't know.

"Now, who's the sports director for CKNW?"

Without fail, everyone knew Big Al, and the sales technique worked every time.

Looking to take advantage of his name recognition and expand beyond broadcasting, Big Al got the idea to use his strong relationship with Canada Safeway to launch a new business venture. Al convinced Tom Milburn, the B.C. regional manager, to assist him in the development of a magazine called *Al Davidson This Week,* which would have the exclusive rights to sell TV listings for Greater Vancouver and Victoria in Safeway stores, at a price of just 10 cents per issue.

Al was a much better sportscaster than he was a businessman and it didn't take long before the fledgling publication was in deep financial trouble. As fate would have it, Al declared bankruptcy approximately the same week that I got fired from my job. I heard through the grapevine that the magazine's printer had inherited the publication when the printing bill went unpaid and while they wished to continue printing it, they weren't interested in becoming the publisher. They needed a publisher.

When you're down, you need to be bold. I heard about the opportunity and approached the new owners to make a deal. I ended up buying 50 per cent of the magazine for the unpaid printing bill of $76,000 and we renamed the publication *TV Week.*

My first day as publisher was April 3, 1976. In a rented back room of a Vancouver print shop, with a staff of just three, we went to work assembling listings, selling advertising, developing editorial material and seeking a network to circulate the "We try harder" TV listings for a market that didn't really need us. When you have *TV Guide*, who needs *TV Week*?

At the time, no one expected that this humble foray into Canadian publishing would put us on a fast track to success. We sold *TV Week* for 10 cents a copy and in the first year our sales topped $70,000. *TV Week* took on a giant and with panache, style and enthusiasm, we began to beat him at his own game. We were local, we were different and we were better. Our initial success spurred new ventures. We began to gather the first recruits of a great army of readers who would nurture Canada Wide Media as a whole into maturity and make it the publishing force that it is today.

Our acquisitions and product development over the last 45 years have established our company as the largest independent publisher in Western Canada and our $20-million company employs more than 50 media professionals and a host of talented freelancers.

TV Week has become one of the highest paid-circulation entertainment and lifestyle magazines in Canada and is still one of our most profitable publications. From our beginning with one little title, we now publish 10 self-owned magazines (including *BCBusiness, Vancouver Magazine, Award Magazine* and *Western Living*) and 20 custom publications for leading clients serving business, consumer, leisure and trade markets. We have also diversified the company to include graphic design, web publishing, direct marketing, book publishing and fundraising.

Was it easy? Of course not! Has everything we've done been entirely successful? No, it hasn't. But that's what being in business is all about – being able to revel in the successes and sweat through the difficulties, learning from our failures, mistakes and bad decisions to eventually make the company stronger and more successful in the future. There were good years and bad years, but we toughed it out. I bought out my original partner years ago and I'm proud to say that Canada Wide is 100 per cent owned by my family 45 years later.

Looking back, I never would have imagined that losing the job I'd staked my future on – something that was completely devastating at the time – would lead me to an opportunity that shaped the rest of my life. I have to say, I am eternally thankful for that particular failure.

So, if there's one lesson that I could pass on to you it would be this: Very often we wait for the right moment to make a change or embark on a new venture . . . and we wait, and we wait and we wait.

Whatever you're waiting for, stop waiting!

Stop waiting until your car or your home is paid off.

Stop waiting until you get in shape or lose 20 pounds.

Stop waiting until you have kids or until your kids leave home.

Stop waiting until you get married, or divorced, or until you retire . . .

Today is the moment you've been waiting for, there is no tomorrow.

So, when should you call the customer?

Today!

When should you praise the employee who did a good job?

Today!

When should you fire the incompetent employee?

Today!

When should you start the exercise program?

Today! (Start with a walk around the block.)

When should you start reading books on leadership, motivation and improving your life?

Today!

When should you do anything worth doing to improve yourself, your relationship or your business?

Today!

It's your life, live it for you and don't forget the 18-40-60 rule:

When you're 18, you worry about what people are saying about you.

When you're 40, you don't care what people say about you.

When you're 60, you realize nobody was talking about you anyway.

So just do it!!!

CHAPTER 15

MORE THAN ONE KIND OF BANK ACCOUNT

"We learned about honesty and integrity – that
the truth matters . . . that you don't take shortcuts or play
by your own set of rules . . . and success
doesn't count unless you earn it fair and square."
– Michelle Obama

Having spoken to audiences on five continents and after delivering 5,000 speeches, it still amazes me how many people ask me to define success.

Most people relate success to wealth and the amount of money and possessions they have accumulated in their lifetime. In other words, many determine that success is about the size of their bank account.

Not to diminish the importance of a growing bank account,

but in my estimation that alone does not dictate your success as a human being. I believe the way you treat others says a lot more about your true worth than your bank balance does and that we all have two kinds of bank accounts, one that is financial and another that is moral.

Success is a byproduct of the character traits you develop over your lifetime and to be truly successful, you need to invest in your relationships, particularly with your spouse/partner, your children and grandchildren, and your community.

Are you a person of your word?

Although they are both billionaires and incredibly successful business magnates, what I admire most about industrialist Jimmy Pattison and my mentor of 50-plus years Joe Segal is that when either of them says they will do something, they just do it! Both men are completely trustworthy in every aspect of their lives, which is something I think we all should aspire to.

The characteristics of honesty, integrity, honouring commitments and personal discipline are so important to our success in life.

In Clayton M. Christensen's book *How Will You Measure Your Life?* the author explains that when it comes to principles and integrity, it is easier to hold to your principles 100 per cent of the time than it is to hold to them 98 per cent of the time. Telling yourself that it's OK to lie, cheat or steal "just this once" is a slippery slope that more often than not leads to a place you don't want to end up. Case in point is a story that recently made headlines around the world when a U.S. judge sentenced President Donald Trump's personal attorney Michael Cohen to three years in prison for tax evasion, bank fraud, campaign finance violations and lying to Congress. The 36-month sentence handed down by Judge William H. Pauley III was accompanied by a $50,000 fine and an order to pay $1.4 million in restitution as well as the forfeiture of $500,000 in assets.

In his deliberation, the judge said, "Each of the crimes involved deception and each appears to have been motivated by personal gain and ambition."

Do you think Michael Cohen has regrets?

I have never met him personally but I know that his wife, children and other family members suffer along with him. Do you think this was the legacy that he wished to pass along to them?

The success we all seek is derived from living every day to the very best of our abilities and making a conscious choice.

As Christensen explains, "You can make a decision that you will lead your life following certain principles, but it's a very different thing to have that conviction in your heart." The challenge of life is an unending stream of extenuating circumstances. Over and over again, you're going to see a grey area in front of you and your instinct is, "Just this once, it's OK if I don't follow the rule." You're constantly confronted with opportunities not to follow the standard that you set for yourself, and you can end up with a very different life than you intended.

Character Is an Inside Job

When it comes to character, there are three things I have learned from experience:

1. It is a waste of time trying to correct other people's mistakes. As a leader and a role model, it is important for you to set an example, but after that, it is up to each individual whether they choose to follow the example or not.
2. You can't change someone else, even someone who is very close to you. People only change if they want to and each person must change themselves.
3. People are generally the way they are because they want to be and that goes for you and me: we choose to be who we are.

The bottom line is, people choose their own character and although there is no end to the excuses we can come up with for why we would lie, cheat, steal, slack off, drink too much, take drugs, abuse our bodies or any number of other destructive behaviours, ultimately we do things because we want to.

What will you do with your life?

Choose carefully. The decisions you make today could have a profound effect on your career, the quality of your personal relationships and most importantly, what you see when you look in the mirror. My mentor Ray Addington, who was president of Kelly Douglas Co. Ltd., often told me, "Not only must you do the right thing, but you must be seen to do the right thing."

If we choose to do the wrong thing, sooner or later it comes back to sting us – and sometimes it's a very big sting. Remember

Bernie Madoff, the guy with the $50-billion Ponzi scheme? He's currently serving a 150-year prison sentence. That's the longest sentence they could give him. He wanted to be remembered as a titan of Wall Street, instead he will be remembered as the biggest fraud of his time. Who knows what Madoff sees when he looks in the mirror, but I can't imagine it's a happy face smiling back. In a recent interview, Madoff's lawyer said that his wife Ruth stopped visiting him years ago and none of his grandchildren have come to see him since he's been in prison.

> When you are the leader, the way you treat people sets the tone for everyone else. If you care about others, they are much more likely to care about you, your business, your goals and your customers.

Sometimes it takes years, even decades, for character to catch up, but when it does, it wipes out everything good that came before. Consider these names as examples:

- O.J. Simpson
- Alan Eagleson (who was stripped of his Order of Canada and resigned from the Hockey Hall of Fame)
- Bill Cosby
- Ben Johnson

Author John Maxwell says, "There is no such thing as business ethics . . . it's all ethics!"

When you have integrity and hold yourself to a high standard of behaviour, all of the other values such as honesty, loyalty, respect, accountability and compassion naturally come along with it and you will find these traits attract people to you, engender trust and make them want to do business. When you compromise integrity, whether it's the result of ego, greed, booze, drugs or illicit sex, a reputation that may have taken 25 years to build can easily be destroyed in five minutes. Guard your reputation, it's the one thing that will follow you no matter where you go.

Another important principle to remember is that what we give out is what we get back. Send out anger, you get it back. Disrespect others and disrespect will soon come your way. Smile and some will look the other way because they think you're crazy, but most will smile back and share in the sense of goodwill.

Some of the most revered business leaders aren't just admired for their business acumen, they are also famous for treating people with respect. Southwest Airlines CEO Herb Kelleher was renowned for his frequent visits to flight crews, where he called employees by name and stopped to chat with them. During his time as Google CEO, Larry Page (who is now CEO of Alphabet, Google's parent company) also strove to maintain an open culture with employees, and every week "Googlers" had an opportunity to ask questions directly to Page and other executives about anything related to the company.

When you are the leader, the way you treat people sets the tone for everyone else. If you care about others, they are much more likely to care about you, your business, your goals and your customers. Over time, the tone you set will filter through to every aspect of your enterprise. Therefore, only send out into the world that which you hope to receive in return.

*"When you are able to maintain your own
highest standards of integrity – regardless of what others
may do – you are destined for greatness."*
– Napoleon Hill

CHAPTER 16

NOT YOUR AVERAGE JOE

"The common traits among all successful people
are desire, determination and confidence."
– Joe Segal

I first met Joe Segal almost 60 years ago. I was selling radio time for CJOR and Joe had a Fields department store at Hastings and Abbott Street in Vancouver, on the corner right across from Woodward's.

I was 19 years old and CJOR Radio hotliner Pat Burns was the No. 1 talk show host in the city, while the very funny Monty McFarlane was the top morning man. It was an up-and-coming station and I was proud to be on its sales force. My sales manager, Arnie Nelson, sent me down there to sell Joe an advertising campaign.

"I'm going to give you the Fields account," he told me. "The guy you're going to see is Joe Segal, but you better do your homework or he'll eat you alive."

While I was a brash young man, I was a bit intimidated by the prospect of being eaten alive. So, shiny briefcase in hand, I plucked up all of my courage and went off to sell a radio campaign to Joe Segal.

When I arrived at Fields, Joe invited me into his little office in the back of the store. One thing I noticed was that

> Maybe a less thickheaded kid would have given up or tried a different approach. Not me.

the door to his office was always open. Joe didn't believe in putting barriers between himself and his employees. It's something that I made note of because it speaks to the character of the man.

Joe was very courteous and he listened to my entire spiel, paying very close attention to everything I had to say but at the end of my presentation, he said in a very straightforward manner, "I'm not going to buy that."

"No sale," I thought to myself as I made my way out of his office. "But at least he didn't eat me alive."

As Joe escorted me from the store, I stopped at a table that was piled high with pajamas. I needed a new pair, so I stopped to take a closer look. On the package of the pajamas were the words "shrink resistant" and I turned to Joe and quipped, "Either these pajamas shrink or they don't, which is it?"

I came back the next month and Joe let me go through my

bag of tricks once again before telling me, "No, I'm not going to buy that either."

Maybe a less thickheaded kid would have given up or tried a different approach. Not me.

I kept returning to pitch advertising to Joe for six months and he never bought anything, yet he did say to me, "Peter, I admire your persistence and you're a pretty good salesman but I'm not going to buy anything from you."

I said, "If I'm that good Joe, how come you're not buying?"

"I'm not buying because you sell me what you want me to buy, but you've never asked me once yet what my needs are. You haven't been interested in me."

It was a great lesson and it changed my sales career right then and there.

I kept going back to visit Joe, even after I moved on from the radio station and eventually started my own company, Canada Wide Media Ltd.

From that moment on, Joe and I hit it off and I have listened closely to all the advice he's been kind enough to offer these past five decades.

CHAPTER 17

GOOD LEADERS

*"A good leader inspires people to have
confidence in the leader. Great leaders inspire people
to have confidence in themselves."*
– Eleanor Roosevelt

I am often asked, "Is leadership acquired or are you born a leader?"

To some degree, I think both are possible. Nevertheless, your ongoing accomplishments are directly related to your level of leadership, so from my point of view leadership skills are something that should be practised every day and developed so that you're always growing and becoming a better leader. With that said, the No. 1 quality of leadership is integrity; without it, being a good leader is almost impossible. John Maxwell once said, "Everything rises and falls on leadership."

And leadership is all about influence.

Regardless of your present position in your organization, your long-term effectiveness will be measured by the level of leadership you demonstrate, so your first job as a leader is to find meaning in the work you are doing and to do more than what you are paid to do. If you keep your eyes open and seize upon every opportunity to learn, to serve and do more than is asked, pretty soon you will be paid for everything you do and your opportunities (as well as your responsibilities) will grow.

As a former commander of the International Space Station, Col. Chris Hadfield knows a thing or two about leadership.

"Ultimately, leadership is not about glorious crowning acts," he said. "It's about keeping your team focused on a goal and motivated to do their best to achieve it, especially when the stakes are high and the consequences really matter. It is about laying the groundwork for others' success and then standing back and letting them shine."

According to Hadfield, as a leader, "The greatest gift you can give to somebody is an essential fundamental belief in a purpose within themselves, something that helps give them guidance in the distance – something to help make the small decisions in their life."

The founder of the National Speakers Association, Cavett Robert, is noted for saying, "About three billion people on the face of the Earth go to bed hungry every night, but four billion people go to bed every night hungry for a word of encouragement and recognition." Make sure your spouse, child, grandchild and people you work with are not among them. Only you can decide that. Everyone has big dreams, hopes, aspirations and mountains to climb. Be the person who encourages people around you with a word of praise or affirmation. Be the inspiration that people need. It only takes 10 seconds, but your words could change someone's life.

> *"Leadership is not something you do to people,*
> *it is something you do for people."*
> – Ken Blanchard

Here are 10 more leadership ideas to help you on your journey:

Learn to listen
As a leader, the ability to listen to the expectations, plans and hopes of employees, customers and stakeholders in an active, thoughtful and critical way is essential. Active listening requires you to ask questions, challenge opinions and request clarifications. Being thoughtful means not jumping to conclusions. It also means setting aside your own biases and giving due consideration to the ideas of others. Being able to listen critically allows you to identify potential areas of conflict before they become major problems. Think of listening as a learning opportunity. After all, how will you understand what people need from you as a leader if you are not listening?

Add a personal touch to your leadership style

Day-to-day life is hectic, especially in the business world, but that's no excuse for not taking the time to get to know the people who work for you and with you. Making a personal investment of your time will pay off. When you venture beyond perfunctory "hellos" to heartfelt greetings, you send out a message of acceptance that will encourage people to open up and share both their ideas and their talent for the benefit of all.

Give direction

Leadership is never given, but leadership is always recognized. The world is in need of leaders, as are communities, countries, businesses, provinces and families. When you give direction to your colleagues, your clients, your employees or your children, you are telling them you believe in their capabilities and what they can achieve. Once you give direction, get out of the way and let people perform.

Good manners never go out of style

Be courteous to all around you, regardless of rank or position. Manners are a way of communicating respect, and everyone deserves respect. In a major survey of corporations, the most common complaint of support personnel was the failure on the part of management to acknowledge their presence other than to issue orders. It is a culture of caring, as well as common courtesy, that helps to bond a team. As a leader, you are always "on stage" modelling behaviour to those you lead. Remember to smile and make eye contact when you are speaking with someone, and that it only takes a moment to say "thank you" for a job well done.

You don't always get what you want

You work hard and deserve recognition, right? Unfortunately, life won't always hand you what you deserve. Sometimes you have to persevere, even when awards and praise don't come your way. Perhaps you weren't nominated for entrepreneur of the year or employee of the month when you thought you should be – don't let that stop you. Don't pursue recognition. Pursue excellence.

Labels are for products, not people

The labels you stamp on another person will not only characterize your relationship with that person, in many instances, if you have power and they don't, it will also limit their potential for development. Therefore, be cautious of thinking, "Hey, she's just an assistant." Keep in mind, people move in many different circles.

> Be courteous to all around you, regardless of rank or position. Manners are a way of communicating respect, and everyone deserves respect.

For instance, although an assistant may not have status in your company, that same assistant may be on the board of directors for a community organization and their expertise could be very useful to your organization. Likewise, an attitude of "I don't have to do that, I'm the boss" in regards to less glamorous tasks limits your opportunity to gain perspective and develop a "can do" work environment. No job is beneath a true leader.

Holding out for a hero

A hero is someone who triumphs over a great challenge – and through their actions, makes the world a better place. Don't underestimate the potential of anyone on your team. When the pressure is on, any one of them may be the hero who rises to the occasion. It is easy to rely on your "best people" when it's time for action, but remember, today's rookie could, and should, be tomorrow's star performer. That will only happen if you provide them opportunities to test themselves.

Oh Lord, it's hard to be humble

Many of the modern-day leaders we look up to are anything but humble, especially if you set your "leader metre" to today's sports personalities. With the multimillion-dollar salaries come egos to match. The problem with ego is it leaves no room for growth and rather than being a role model for young people, it makes you a target for those who would like to see you fail.

According to Steven Covey in *First Things First*, "Humility is truly the mother of all virtues. It makes us a vessel, a vehicle, an agent, instead of 'the source' or the principal. It unleashes all other learning, all growth and progress."

This can be a difficult concept for many leaders to grasp.

People often rise to leadership positions by the sheer force of their personality and/or intellect and they are accustomed to wielding power over others. Thus they tend to have outsized egos, which on the surface seems to be the opposite of humility. But having a healthy sense of self does not mean you cannot be humble, nor does it mean that you cannot project strength. History provides many examples of great leaders who were both humble and strong: Jesus Christ or Dr. Martin Luther King, for instance.

In leadership, strive to be a person that you yourself could look up to. Mohandas K. Gandhi put it clearly: "It is unwise to be too sure of one's own wisdom. It is healthy to be reminded that the strongest might weaken and the wisest might err."

Never turn down the opportunity to learn from others
I read a story recently about a fellow who takes this philosophy seriously. Whenever he has a few idle moments with another person, whether it is a child, adult, customer, business associate, close friend, acquaintance or even a stranger waiting for the elevator, he makes this request of them, "Teach me something." He says it is amazing what you can learn standing in the checkout line at the grocery store. "Older ladies know all sorts of things that I don't," he says.

Life is a laboratory of leadership
All too often we look to a university or MBA program to teach us about leadership when, in fact, life is a veritable laboratory of

leadership. If you are just willing to take the time to stop and pay attention, the people you meet every day have wisdom to offer. There are many types of leader – the conductor of the orchestra, the coach, the community organizer and the visionary, to name just a few. We can learn from all of them. During my lifetime, I have spent many years at school, attended dozens of seminars, read hundreds of books and been introduced to thousands of terrific people. I acquired leadership skills from all of them, but it is the *people* I remember the most. Don't forget, in addition to being a leader, you are also a teacher, friend, role model and mentor. Play each part to its potential.

CHAPTER 18

NOT ADEQUATE

"One key to success is demanding more
than adequacy, never settling for good enough
and always doing a little bit more."
– Michael Josephson

In Eugene H. Peterson's book *As Kingfishers Catch Fire*, he recounts a story he read in the *New York Times* about a British gentleman who had purchased his first Rolls-Royce.

Try as he might, the man could find nothing in the advertising material, the owner's manual or on the automobile itself that told him of the engine's horsepower.

Upon making inquiries, he learned it was not the policy of the Rolls-Royce Corporation to talk about the horsepower of their vehicles.

This man, though, was curious and having paid a rather

substantial purchase price, thought he was entitled to know what the horsepower was.

So he wrote the company and asked them to provide this piece of information.

In a few days, a telegram was delivered to his house with a one-word answer, "ADEQUATE."

"That may be sufficient for Rolls-Royce, one of the most prestigious motor companies in the world," I thought as I read the story, but it struck me that, particularly as we approach the final years of our lives, "adequate" is not enough.

When this book is published, not so long after my 77th birthday, I know I will have more life behind me than before me.

I once asked my family doctor what my life expectancy was and we both agreed that 90 years old (give or take a few years) would be a good expectation.

> At my funeral, do I want to be called adequate – or is there a more positive, and hopefully even accurate, way to sum up my life and my God-given talents.

That is just 13 years (or 676 weeks) from now. It doesn't sound nearly long enough, but that's reality.

And as I ponder this reality, the question I ask myself often is, "How do I want to be remembered?"

Does "adequate" fit the bill?

An adequate husband, father, grandfather, business leader, speaker, community leader, boss . . . you get the idea!

At my funeral, do I want to be called adequate – or is there a more positive, and hopefully even accurate, way to sum up my life and my God-given talents.

Never Settle for Good Enough

On the wall of Jimmy Pattison's office, there is part of a poem by James Russell Lowell that his mother gave him:

> *Life is a sheet of paper white*
> *Whereon each one of us may write*
> *His word or two, and then comes night.*
> *Greatly begin! Tho thou have time*
> *But for a line, be that sublime,*
> *Not failure, but low aim is crime.*

Good enough isn't necessarily a bad thing. In many areas of life, chasing perfection is a fool's errand, or at least a poor use of our time. We don't need to spend hours taste-testing every salad dressing on the supermarket shelf to find the absolute best; a good enough brand will usually work just fine for our side dish. The problems start when this "good enough" attitude spills over into the things we say and do.

I interviewed music magnate David Foster for the *BCBusiness* Top 100 event in June 2017.

Here are a few of David's thoughts from that conversation that really resonated with me:

"Ideas flow through you not from you."

"People talk about luck but I don't believe in luck. I actually believe luck is when hard work meets opportunity . . . if you're prepared and an opportunity comes along; something good is going to happen for sure."

"When I went into the studio, I watched the producers very carefully in every session I was in. I was studying what that job was because I wanted that job – I wanted the producer job and I got it!"

"It's not in my nature to give up . . . that's the entrepreneurial spirit. I don't just want to be a 'gun for hire,' I want to own the things I create."

"I try to be great every day and most days I'm only good, but I keep shooting for that greatness every single day."

"You give me something with your name on it and you make excuses for it?" That was the response of producer Quincy Jones after David gave him his record to review with a note of caution about the lack of quality on some of the songs.

"Ever since that day," says David, "I have never, ever, ever not tried to be great again, because good is the enemy of great."

CHAPTER 19

THE LAW OF RECIPROCITY

My third book, *It Begins With a Dream*, was published in 1996 and dedicated to my mother, Winnifred Ivy Legge. While those in my business and social circles might guess that my father was my primary role model as a young man, I had an incredibly strong bond with my mother and it was mom who influenced my life's direction more than any other as she challenged, supported and occasionally shoved me in the right directions.

I learned many practical things from my mother about how to get along with others. One of the most useful lessons she passed on was the universal law of reciprocity.

What is reciprocity? According to Wikipedia, in social psychology, reciprocity is a social norm of responding to a positive action with another positive action, rewarding kind actions. In other words, individuals are more inclined to do favours for people who once did something nice for them. What's more, when they return the favour, the value of their "payback" is often greater than the original good deed.

"Something as simple as opening the door for someone or getting someone a cup of coffee is a very powerful technique that you can use to cause people to like you and to feel obligated to you," says leadership guru Brian Tracy. "Successful people are always looking for opportunities to help others. Unsuccessful people are always asking, 'What's in it for me?'"

As someone who believes in reciprocity, I tend to say "thank you" a lot. I also write a lot of thank-you letters and make sure I express my appreciation when people go out of their way to help me. But the most effective way to use reciprocity, particularly in the business world, is to be the one to initiate it. Here's a story to illustrate my point:

I once tried to make a sale to a man named David Bentall. You may recognize the name; his family built a lot of Downtown Vancouver and their name still graces the iconic Bentall Centre. Despite my best sales tactics, David wasn't buying; however, partway through my pitch, he said to me; "You know, I want to do something for my father. He's 80 years old and he's been recognized with the Order of Canada among other honours, but my efforts to do more have been denied by the board members. They say we can't spend any more money on public demonstration."

I was well aware of the substantial philanthropic contributions that David's father Clarke had made to the Vancouver community and, as a member of the board of Variety Club, I decided to submit his name as a candidate for the Variety Club Golden Heart Achievement Award, the highest honour Variety Club bestows.

I was delighted when his nomination was accepted.

Not surprisingly, I was asked to chair the event that would be held to honour Clarke, and for a year I met with David every Wednesday to plan the dinner, sell tickets for the event and arrange the entertainment. We lined up the incomparable Bob Hope as the principal performer and organized a number of other speakers.

The event was a wonderful celebration and through our combined efforts, we raised $160,000 for Variety's special kids. What's more, in the course of planning the event, I had found a new friend in David Bentall. I felt more than satisfied with the outcome of my gesture; however, three months later, David asked if I could meet him for breakfast.

"Absolutely!" I responded, suddenly remembering that I still hadn't been able to sell him an ad for any of our magazines.

We sat down for breakfast and after catching up on current events, David said to me, "I just want to thank you sincerely for what you did for my father."

> As someone who believes in reciprocity, I tend to say "thank you" a lot. I also write a lot of thank-you letters and make sure I express my appreciation when people go out of their way to help me.

"The pleasure was ours," I said. "We did it for your dad, but we also did it for Variety's special-needs kids."

"There's something else . . . " said David.

I brightened, and while I hadn't asked for it, I sensed that a sale was imminent.

"Somewhere during our year of planning, you said you were fascinated by Prince Charles and Diana."

"I am," I said. "They appear to be quite charming."

"How would you like to have dinner with them?" he asked.

"I . . . "

He extended his hand, "Here are two plane tickets to Toronto for you and your wife. You'll be having dinner with Prince Charles and Diana, Princess of Wales."

I gulped, "Can I call him Chuck?"

I was absolutely thrilled. The law of reciprocity had worked on the grandest of scales.

CHAPTER 20

EMBRACE YOUR FAILURES AND MOVE ON

"You can't outwit fate by standing on the sidelines
placing little side bets about the outcome of life . . .
if you don't play you can't win."
– Judith McNaught

W hy do some people succeed and others don't? Is it because some are luckier than others or is it simply because others moved on and did better after they failed? There is more to failure than you think.

Failure, like success, is not permanent. But both are part of life. Some of the most successful people in the world, who have excelled beyond what most of us could even imagine, are not the most educated or even the most talented. But they are the individuals who are able to stand committed to one goal or purpose come hell or high water. They did not stop at failure.

In my book *The Power of Tenacity – The Three Things You'll Need to Make Your Mark in Life*, I shared the notion that somebody, at some point in your life, has told you to embrace your failures. Most likely, you just shook your head and asked, "Why would I want to do that?" Or maybe you thought to yourself, "That's easy for them to say, they don't have to live with it, I do." And you're absolutely right, but here's what's so good about that.

Failure does not prevent success; just the opposite, in fact: it's a stepping stone to success. By accepting that something has failed and moving on, you'll be able to focus on alternatives that might just lead to a better opportunity. So instead of wallowing in self pity or beating yourself up, here are some practical steps to get back on track when you fail:

1. **Accept that you're human and get over the guilt**
   Everybody fails. They may not all advertise those failures, but trust me, even the people who seem to go from one success to another have had their share of failures. Guilt, shame, embarrassment – these are only helpful in so much as they help you to identify the lessons that can be learned so you can move on and try something else.

2. **Talk it out**
   Find a shoulder to cry on but not just any shoulder; that's

the advice from blogger Lewis Schiff, who wrote the book *Business Brilliant*. Most people don't want to talk about failure because they are ashamed of it, explains Schiff. Which is exactly why you are unlikely to get helpful support and insights from people who haven't faced similar challenges, and that includes family and close friends. These are some things that only others in the same situation

> Failure does not prevent success; just the opposite, in fact: it's a stepping stone to success. By accepting that something has failed and moving on, you'll be able to focus on alternatives that might just lead to a better opportunity.

can understand, so it's better to seek out someone who has been there and done that.

3. **Be honest with yourself**

Once a deal or a project falls apart, track back to figure out what went wrong. Start all the way at the beginning. The acute failures that killed the project right at the end might have only been symptoms of chronic problems that were there from the beginning and just continued to grow. Maybe you were working with the wrong client, in the wrong market or with the wrong team. The real lesson might be about choosing who you work with and the projects you work on more carefully, not about details of the execution that went badly.

4. **Own it**

Don't go looking for others to blame when one of your endeavours goes off the rails, even though they may have had some part to play. Look first at yourself. Did you communicate your expectations clearly? Perhaps you avoided asking difficult questions because you just wanted to close the deal. Or maybe you didn't take the time to find out what was really required. It's easy to blame others when things go wrong but you can't control others, so assume they will remain the same and you're the one who must learn and adjust if you want the next project to be more successful.

5. **Dust yourself off and try again**

Once you've figured out what you can learn from your failure, it's time to get back in the game. Your second attempt at something is always stronger than your first, so don't let the fear of failure hold you back. Fear of failure is actually worse than failure itself, because it condemns you to a life of unrealized potential. So now that you know failure isn't fatal, start using what you've learned. You're older and wiser than you were before and you know a few things to look out for. Use that to your advantage.

CHAPTER 21

STEP OUTSIDE YOUR COMFORT ZONE

*"It is not the mountain we conquer,
but ourselves."*
– Sir Edmund Hillary

I f you've ever been to the top of a mountain, you know how exhilarating it can be when you finally reach the summit. Mountains have a special way of lifting us above the ordinary and allowing us to survey our world from a new and exciting perspective. It's different up there. All the mediocrity seems to drop away and in the clean air we can breathe deeply a world that's fresher and more spiritually connected, where we can rise above the routine and feel our hearts swell with the thrill of achievement.

For obvious reasons, some people will never have a mountaintop experience, because it requires both planning and the intention to start climbing. These are perhaps the same people who believe that everything they desire should be handed to them with no effort on their part. They buy a lottery ticket and sit back and wait for the big moment. And despite that famous marketing slogan, "You never know!" the moment rarely ever does come. Meanwhile, time slips by and life goes on.

Climbing mountains and achieving our dreams have a lot in common; they both require us to step outside of our comfort zone.

The idea of the comfort zone goes back to a classic experiment in psychology. In 1908, psychologists John D. Dodson and Robert M. Yerkes explained that a state of relative comfort creates a steady level of performance. In order to maximize performance, we need to be in a state of relative

> Those who have been to the mountaintop know that it takes effort to get there, but once you've been, you can't wait to challenge yourself to reach the next peak . . .

anxiety – where our stress levels are slightly higher than normal. This state is called "Optimal Anxiety," and it's just outside our comfort zone.

A few benefits of pushing yourself outside the comfort zone:

- You'll be more productive. Without the sense of unease that comes from having deadlines and expectations, we tend to just do what is necessary to get by and we lose the ambition to do more and learn new things. We also use the excuse that we're busy as a way to stay in our comfort zone and avoid trying new things.

- Learning to live outside your comfort zone when you choose to can help prepare you for life changes that force you out of it, making it easier to deal with unexpected changes. Fear and uncertainty are natural, but by taking risks in a controlled way and challenging yourself to things you normally wouldn't, you can practise feeling a little bit uncomfortable.

- Once you start stepping outside your comfort zone it actually gets bigger, so the more you do it the more you *can* do it and the easier it is to push your boundaries in different ways.

- You'll find it easier to harness your creativity. Seeking new experiences and learning new skills opens the door to innovation. A positively uncomfortable experience can help us see old problems from a new perspective and tackle the challenges we face with renewed enthusiasm.

Those who have been to the mountaintop know that it takes effort to get there, but once you've been, you can't wait to challenge yourself to reach the next peak, even if it means more discomfort and more hard work.

CHAPTER 22

TEN TRAITS THAT DEFINE PEOPLE OF INFLUENCE – AND HOW YOU CAN INCREASE YOUR INFLUENCE RIGHT NOW

"Outstanding people have one thing in common:
An absolute sense of mission."
– Zig Ziglar

We all want to be inspired, we all want to be the hero in our own story and we all want to influence others. Influential people are people that others want to listen to. To increase your influence, you need to freely share your skills and insights and you must be passionate in your pursuit of a greater future. Influential people believe that one person really can change the world. They also have these 10 traits:

1. They think for themselves. Influential people aren't just trying to get the job done in the short-term. They have big dreams and ideas of how the world could or should be better. Everything they do is a step towards making this vision a reality.

2. They are proactive. Influential people don't wait for things like new ideas and new technologies to find them; they seek those things out. These early adopters always want to anticipate what's next. They're influential because they see what's coming, and they see what's coming because they look for it. Then they spread the word.

3. They are graciously disruptive. They are the ones who constantly ask, "What if?" and "Why not?" They're not afraid to challenge conventional wisdom but they don't disrupt things for the sake of being disruptive; they do it to make things better. Influencers inspire *everyone* around them to explore new ideas and think differently about their work.

4. They walk the talk. They make sure that their beliefs and aims are reflected in every interaction – and they take pains to avoid contradiction or hypocrisy. Not only does

> Influential people do not react emotionally and defensively to dissenting opinions – they welcome them. They're humble enough to know that they don't know everything . . .

this demonstrate integrity, it helps make sure that their message is reiterated and absorbed, over and over again.

5. They know how to listen. Counterintuitive as it might sound, the best way to influence someone and get them on your side is to ask questions about them and really listen to what they say.

6. They know how to keep their cool. Influential people do not react emotionally and defensively to dissenting opinions – they welcome them. They're humble enough to know that they don't know everything and that someone else might see something they missed. And if that person is right, they embrace the idea wholeheartedly because they care more about the end result than being right.

7. They adapt to the changing world around them. Influential people understand that while their message is constant, the medium is evolving. They get that you need to adopt new technologies and approaches in order to cope with a changing world and stay relevant and effective.

8. They put others at ease. Anyone can cajole others into doing what they want. While it might make you powerful in the short term, it doesn't make you influential, it makes you a bully – and the thing about bullies is, everyone wants them to fail. By inviting contributions from your team and making colleagues feel happy, inspired and excited, you foster a culture of trust and loyalty that drives the endeavour forward. If anything goes wrong, your team has your back.

9. They focus on what really matters. Influential people understand that for a project to be successful, it needs to

stay on track. They're able to cut through the static and clutter, focus on what matters, and point it out to everyone else. This is what truly makes them leaders.

10. They leverage their networks. Influential people know how to make lasting connections. Not only do they know a lot of people, they get to know their connections' connections. More importantly, they add value to everyone in their network. They share advice and know-how, and they make connections between people who should get to know each other.

How to Become More Influential

Influence has a lot to do with emotional intelligence, which is essentially having the awareness that emotions can drive our behaviour, which in turn has an impact on the people around us, whether it is positive or negative. Our level of emotional intelligence determines the degree to which we are able to manage our own behaviour, navigate socially complex situations and make personal decisions that result in positive results for ourselves and others.

Every one of us has the ability to be more aware and increase our influence, if we choose. Here are some tips to help:

Use people's names and remember personal details

Remembering someone's name and using it when you greet them is Influence 101. At a basic level, if someone remembers our name, it means that we have made enough of an impression that they took the time and effort to remember it. The more significant information we can remember about people, the stronger the impression we will make and the more influential we become to them.

Develop listening abilities

Whether or not you agree with someone, realize that they have a need to be heard. In order for them to feel like they have been heard, we need to really listen. One way to improve listening skills is to repeat back to someone in your own words what they have just said. If you're not clear on what they've said, ask questions. Good listening requires us to overcome the urge to think ahead to what we want to say and stay focused on the person who is speaking.

Follow nonverbal cues

When two people are intensely connected in conversation, they tend to mirror each other's nonverbal cues, such as smiling, leaning into the conversation and making a great deal of eye contact. Because they demonstrate our interest and engagement, these actions make the person we are speaking with more open to our ideas and influence. When you give your full attention to an interaction, the person you're engaging with is much more likely to feel that you understand them.

Ask for input

The next time someone asks you for advice or assistance, notice how it makes you feel. Everyone has an area of knowledge or expertise that they are proud of, and asking them to share it is an indication that you value their expertise.

Respond rather than react

Influential people have a unique ability to handle criticism when it comes to their own mistakes or when dealing with someone else who has made a mistake. Rather than reacting emotionally, influential people tend to take a moment to reflect and think before they respond to criticism or offer a critique of their own. Understanding that relationships are easier to maintain than they are to repair and keeping in mind our own interdependence with those around us can help in this regard.

Recognize other people's accomplishments

Everyone appreciates being acknowledged for something they did well. Tipping your cap to another's accomplishments will ensure that you're remembered positively and will make you stand out from others who don't notice good work. Of course, it's important to be sincere in the acknowledgement. If you're perceived to be superficial or phony, it's more likely to damage the relationship.

Hone your conflict-resolution skills

When you work as part of a team, conflict will inevitably arise, but conflict itself isn't necessarily negative. According to Martha Schmitz, a senior adviser at Mentat, "Conflict offers teams the opportunity to consider new ideas, challenge themselves and grow. However, it is important that differences of opinion are not allowed to fester and cause ongoing anger, tension or bitterness between colleagues. The ability to openly talk about conflict, facilitate difficult conversations between colleagues, help people feel heard and find a way to reach consensus are of great importance to strong team functioning."

The best way to get better at conflict resolution is to actively work on it when opportunities arise.

"There's no way to know how many people
your life will influence. You don't know who is watching,
listening or learning from you."
– Charles Stanley

CHAPTER 23

THE AMAZING CHARLIE PLUMB

"Life doesn't get easier or more
forgiving, we get stronger and more resilient."
– Steve Maraboli

C apt. Charles Plumb was a U.S. Navy jet pilot in Vietnam. On his 75th combat mission, his plane was destroyed by a surface-to-air missile. Plumb ejected and parachuted into enemy hands. He spent the next six years in a communist prison in Vietnam. Miraculously, he survived the ordeal and now lectures on lessons learned from that experience.

One day, years after his return to the U.S., Capt. Plumb and his wife were in a restaurant when a man who had been sitting at another table came up and pointed at Charlie, "You're Plumb!" he said. "You flew jet fighters in Vietnam from the aircraft carrier *Kitty Hawk*. You were shot down!"

"How in the world did you know that?" asked Charlie.

"I packed your parachute," the man replied.

Charlie gasped in surprise.

The man pumped his hand and said, "I guess it worked!"

A grateful Charlie assured him, "It sure did. If your chute hadn't worked, I wouldn't be here today."

Charlie couldn't sleep that night as he thought about the fellow he'd met.

"I kept wondering what he had looked like in a Navy uniform: a white hat, a bib in the back, and bell-bottom trousers," said Charlie. "I wondered how many times I might have seen him around before that fateful day and not even said, 'Good morning, how are you?' or anything at all because, you see, I was a fighter pilot and he was just a sailor."

He thought of the many hours the sailor had spent at a long wooden table in the bowels of the ship, carefully weaving the shrouds and folding the silks of each chute, holding in his hands each time the fate of someone he didn't know.

Now when he's doing a presentation, Charlie asks his audience, "Who's packing your parachute?" Everyone has someone (usually it's more than just one person) who provides what they require to make it through the day.

Furthermore, Charlie points out that he needed many kinds of parachutes when his plane was shot down over enemy territory – he needed his physical parachute, his mental parachute, his emotional parachute and his spiritual parachute.

He called on all these supports before his ordeal was over. Sometimes in the daily challenges that life gives us, we miss what is really important. We may fail to say hello, please and thank you, to congratulate someone on something wonderful that has happened to them, to give a compliment or just do something nice for no reason. As you go through this week, this month, this year, take time to recognize all of the people who pack your parachutes and be thankful for them.

Moral of the story: There are many people who influence our lives without us knowing it, and it is worthwhile to be grateful and look kindly on those who choose to take on a service role. Many of us live a life of convenience and sometimes it can be easy to forget just how much we have and how many people have a hand in that everyday comfort (as well as the well-being of those we love). When is the last time you really acknowledged someone like your:

- barista
- housecleaner
- childcare worker
- dog walker
- teacher
- boss
- co-workers
- convenience store clerk
- gas station attendant

> There are many people who influence our lives without us knowing it, and it is worthwhile to be grateful and look kindly on those who choose to take on a service role.

As I mentioned at the start of this chapter, today Charlie Plumb is a world-renowned speaker, sharing his story of inspiration and hope with audiences of all ages. One of the questions that comes up over and over again is, "How did you survive six years as a prisoner of war?"

Charlie believes that positive thinking had a lot to do with it. In one of his TED Talks, he shared the results of a study about how our attitude towards stress impacts life expectancy. The study followed 29,000 people who were middle-aged or older for eight years. At the beginning of the study, they asked participants to describe what kind of stress they had in their life and how it impacted them. Some people said that stress had a negative impact on their life and a number even went so far as to say that stress was killing them. On the other end of the spectrum, there were those who said things like, "I find stress energizing, it's motivating and it makes me a better person. After all, it is stress and adrenaline that makes some people into Olympic athletes and superstars."

After eight years, 43 per cent of the people in the study had passed away. The people who thought that stress was negative were the ones who died; while the positive thinkers lived longer than anyone else involved in the experiment.

"That says to me, stress doesn't kill you," deduced Charlie. "It's your perception of the stress that kills you . . . My mother told me early in life, 'Son, every experience in your life will have good and bad. It's like a puzzle, search for the good.'"

When Charlie was shot down and became a PoW, he was beaten and tortured by his captors. As he lay bleeding on the dirt floor of his eight-by-eight prison cell, he struggled to comprehend how he could possibly find anything positive in the situation.

"Mom can't be right," he told himself. "Nothing good will ever come from this experience. At best, this period in my life will be something that I can forget one day."

In his hot, putrid cage somewhere in the middle of the jungle, Charlie Plumb didn't have a window to look out, nor did he have any books to read; he didn't even have a pencil to mark on the wall. For 2,103 days, from the age of 24 to 30, Charlie was alone in a space so small that he could pace just three steps in one direction before turning to pace three steps in the other.

After six years, the war ended and Charlie was one of 591 PoWs who returned to the United States. Unfortunately, by that time, his wife, who had waited more than five years for his return, was engaged to another man.

As he lay in his hospital bed recuperating, he found himself curled up in the fetal position thinking, "This is so terrible, what could be worse than this? This event will never have any value to me. I want nothing more than to forget this pain."

A couple days later, Charlie was asked to speak at a press conference. Afterwards, on the way back up to his hospital room, a young reporter pushed his way into the elevator with

Charlie as the doors closed.

The young man had tears in his eyes as he said, "Mr. Plumb, you really got to me in there. Man, I've had a miserable year, my family is falling apart, my job is terrible, I even wondered if I wanted to go on living, but you've given me hope."

"Suddenly," said Charlie, "I saw some value in my experience, some value in the pain, so I decided to share my story. First, I wrote an autobiography and then I started to speak. I've spoken over 5,000 times, identifying with people who have had the same kinds of challenges I faced and letting them know that they can make the same kinds of choices."

When Charlie and his fellow PoWs returned from Vietnam, everyone expected them to be broken, suffering from post-traumatic stress disorder, but that wasn't the case for the majority of the 591 men. In fact, many of them went on to distinguished careers in the military, business and politics.

"They tell us that today, we're happier and healthier than if we'd never been shot down at all, figure that out," said Charlie. "Life is a choice, regardless of where you go or the challenges you face, you can choose happiness or sadness, you can choose health or sickness, you can choose life or death. I'm convinced that adversity is a horrible thing to waste. There's value in every experience in life.

"Any one of us going through any challenge in life has a choice. We can focus on the bad or negative aspects of the experience or, as my mother taught me, we can look for the good. I choose to look for the good."

"It's a funny thing about life: once you begin
to take note of the things you are grateful for, you begin
to lose sight of the things that you lack."
– Germany Kent

As it happens, Charlie Plumb and I are members of the invitation-only Speakers Roundtable, to which I was inducted in the year 2000. Only 20 active members are part of this organization. We meet twice a year at different locations across North America to get reconnected and discuss our craft; we all share common ground as professional speakers and look to the other members for guidance on the best ways to reach our respective audiences. My own growth as a speaker has been impacted enormously by this think tank, and I'm so very grateful for the opportunity.

CHAPTER 24

WHAT SUCCESSFUL PEOPLE ALREADY KNOW

"You can have everything you want
in life if you help enough other people get
what they want in life."
– Zig Ziglar

The word success is one of the most commonly used in the English language, yet success eludes many people. Why is that?

The hidden secret is this and it determines the sort of success you are working for: "As a man thinketh in his heart, so is he. Men do not attract that which they want, but that which they are." For better or worse, we are the architects of our own lives and we are the recipients of that which we put into the world. Our own thoughts and behaviour determine our success.

The secret of success is not really a secret at all, success is simply the uncommon application of common knowledge. In other words, when it comes to success, what matters isn't so much learning something new but putting into practice what we already know.

Sounds simple enough, doesn't it? Well, in reality it is, provided you approach every day as a challenge and a new opportunity to take positive action.

In his book *The Millionaire Messenger,* author Brendon Burchard points out an important truth about where we put our focus: "If people spent as much time worrying about how to make a difference as they do about how they could make more money, they would soon find themselves rich beyond belief."

Successful people are often just ordinary people, who might be a little hungrier for success but like us all they experience their share of difficult times. Nevertheless they keep pushing through and the word "quit" is not in their vocabulary.

Dr. G. Campbell Morgan tells of a man whose shop burned to the ground in the Great Chicago Fire of 1871. The next morning he arrived to work and set up a little table

> Nobody is great without spending time and effort to develop themselves. Success takes effort and a large part of success is putting in the time each and every day.

with a sign amid the charred ruins. The sign read, *"Everything lost except wife, children and hope. Business as usual tomorrow morning!"*

Once again, successful people know that success isn't about *avoiding* failure, it's about *learning* from failure. Given the number of decisions each of us will make in our lifetime, it stands to reason that not all of them will have the desired outcome, so a degree of failure is to be expected. Don't fear failure, view it as a sign that you need to adjust your approach. Learn from each mistake, then regroup and continue to press forward.

According to Andrew Carnegie, "The average person puts only 25 per cent of his energy and ability into his work. The world takes off its hat to those who put in more than 50 per cent of their capacity and stands on its head for those few-and-far-between souls who devote 100 per cent."

Nobody is great without spending time and effort to develop themselves. Success takes effort and a large part of success is putting in the time each and every day. Getting organized requires effort. Setting goals and making plans to achieve them requires effort. Working through obstacles and staying on track requires effort. People don't fail to succeed, they fail to make the effort to succeed. To succeed in any endeavour, you need to make an effort.

Remember, if everything came easy, we would never know how it feels to want, to dream and to savour the sense of accomplishment and satisfaction that comes with achieving those dreams.

As John Maxwell says, "Leadership is all about influence – the first person you need to influence is you."

John's latest book, which for me has been the most inspiring, is titled *Intentional Living: Choosing a Life That Matters*. It is almost 300 pages, and I read my copy in three days. Towards the end, he talks about two mindsets:

1. Scarcity mindset
2. Abundance mindset

Here's a quick story to illustrate the difference between them:

Imagine that you and I are walking down the street. You breathe in. You breathe out. I breathe in. I breathe out. We both need oxygen to survive. Would you worry that there would not be enough oxygen for both of us? Of course not – air is abundant.

Now imagine we are scuba diving and my tank starts to malfunction. I signal that I need to share the oxygen in your tank. Suddenly the air becomes a precious commodity. Its scarcity makes us worry. What if there isn't enough for both of us?

Our attitude towards scarcity and abundance in all aspects of life greatly influences our overall success. Those who live with a scarcity mindset are often plagued by fear, stress and anxiety and feel a need to compete with others, even when there is abundance. Alternatively, those who live with an abundance mindset believe that there is always more of everything in life, whether it relates to money, relationships, resources, opportunities or recognition.

According to John, having an abundance mindset opens up possibilities, options, alternatives and creativity.

I know which mindset I choose to have. How about you?

"People who are unwilling to grow
will never reach their potential."
– John Maxwell

CHAPTER 25

LESSONS LEARNED THE HARD WAY

"Maybe you needed to get whacked hard by life before you understood what you wanted out of it."
– Jodi Picoult

L ife's crossroads, despite the difficulties they present, create opportunities for change. The choices we make can either help us grow and improve, or stifle us and knock us down. The life lessons we learn during times of hardship are 10 times more abundant than when things are going our way. And though they may be hard to swallow, that doesn't mean they aren't valuable. Here are a few lessons I learned the hard way:

Things are never as bad as they seem
Bad things happen to good people; in fact, they happen to

everyone, and usually for no particular reason. After I had a stroke in my 60s, a significant part of my body was paralyzed and I struggled to see how I would ever recover. I couldn't imagine a life where I was unable to be a speaker, it was the thing I loved to do most in the world. Eventually, I had to accept that my recovery might be slow and it was going to take a lot of hard work. I also came to realize that it is the person who's able to put things in proper perspective and get on with life that eventually succeeds, even if life ends up looking quite different from what it once was. When you have been through a tough time or two, you start to realize that you are more resilient than you thought and no matter what happens, you can, and will, go on.

Life's too unpredictable for rigid expectations

When you stop expecting things to be a certain way, you can appreciate them for what they are. Life's greatest gifts are rarely wrapped the way you expect them to be, but with a positive attitude and an open mind, you will find that even though things don't always happen when and how you intend, it isn't a bad thing; it's actually what makes life interesting.

It never hurts to ask

When your best friend asks out the person of your dreams and they say yes, you will regret not voicing your interest. When someone gets the promotion you wanted, you will regret not asking for it first. And when someone breaks your heart, you will regret not asking why. Life is short and opportunity doesn't like to wait around. Not asking for what you want is far more painful in the long run than overcoming the fear of rejection – but you probably won't fully appreciate this wisdom until you watch what you want slip away, or worse yet, go to someone else.

> It is easier to travel, experiment and take risks when you are younger . . . It's also easier to recover from a mistake and apply the valuable lessons those mistakes provide.

You don't have to live your life the way others expect you to

Your work is going to fill a large part of your life and the only way to be truly satisfied is to do what you believe is great work – which means you need to love what you do. If you haven't found it yet, keep looking. Don't settle. As with all matters of the heart, you'll know when you find it. So keep looking, and don't be afraid to go in a new direction. Life is so much easier when you live it for yourself.

Don't wait

The older you get, the more complicated life is and the less likely you are to spontaneously do the things you dream about. It is easier to travel, experiment and take risks when you are younger and have fewer responsibilities. It's also easier to recover from a mistake and apply the valuable lessons that mistake provides.

It takes consistent effort and practise to become an expert

There is no elevator to success; you have to take the stairs. People usually get discouraged when it requires more time than they thought to master a skill or climb the ladder of success within their chosen career. Having a university degree doesn't make you an expert, you need to pay your dues. On average, it takes 10,000 hours of practise to truly master a skill, so there's no time to waste, get a move on!

"The difference between school and life?
In school, you're taught a lesson and then given a test.
In life, you're given a test that teaches you a lesson."
– Tom Bodett

CHAPTER 26

LIFE LONG LEARNING

"Learning never exhausts the mind."
– Leonardo da Vinci

I n the '90s, I decided to go back to university. This time, it was Disney University in Florida.

The one-week course was called "The Disney Approach to People Management."

It was an in-depth seminar that centred on the fundamental elements of Disney corporate culture and how to inspire and motivate your employees.

On the very first day, our Disney University instructor shared this quote: "I may be only one person but I can be one person that makes a difference."

Walt Disney, visionary that he was, knew it would take thousands of people to deliver the magical experience he envisioned for his guests and the only way to engender the necessary enthusiasm in his team was to win their hearts and minds. As a leader, he believed that good ideas could come from anywhere within an organization and therefore it was important to build relationships with employees at all levels.

> Walt Disney knew that you can imagine and even construct the most wonderful place in the world, but it takes people to make and keep that dream a reality.

Out of this philosophy comes the Walt Disney Workers Success Formula:

Quality Cast Experience + Quality Guest Experience + Quality Business Practices = The Future

Given that 64 per cent of Disney guests are repeat customers, the approximate 38,000 cast members (that's what employees of Disney are called) have an important role to play in delivering a consistently excellent experience.

I appreciate the way the founder of the company placed so much importance on his employees, who he understood to be his greatest asset.

Walt Disney himself said, "The growth and development of the Walt Disney Company is directly related to the growth and development of its human resources – our cast."

True, a company can only thrive with the right people. And when our employees are happy because we treat them right, they will be happy not just to treat our customers the way we ask them to, but to treat them even better.

Walt Disney knew that you can imagine and even construct the most wonderful place in the world, but it takes *people* to make and keep that dream a reality.

Here are six more lessons that we can learn from Walt Disney's example about how to succeed in business and in life:

Be fearless when it comes to selling yourself (and your ideas)
Halfway through making *Snow White*, Walt Disney ran out of money to finish the film that had been termed by many as "Disney's folly." Even his own family begged him to give it up, but Disney was not dissuaded. He personally travelled to different producers and showed them the raw footage and convinced them to finish financing the picture. Upon its release, *Snow White* became an instant success and ushered in the golden age of animation.

Leadership requires inspiration
Walt Disney had a unique ability to hire people who were more talented than he was and inspire them to work towards a common goal. Most often, he accomplished this through storytelling; he was an incredible storyteller. It's one thing to tell your employees to do something, it's another to inspire them to action. When Walt shared his vision for the future of Disney, he would go into elaborate detail and he made his workers an integral part of the story, inspiring them to push harder and strive for excellence, no matter what their role.

Always be improving

Following the success of *Snow White* and other feature-length Disney films including *Cinderella*, *Alice in Wonderland* and *Fantasia*, Walt Disney could have rested on his laurels, but that wasn't his style. Instead, he completely switched gears and set out to build an amusement park where parents and children could have fun together. Once Disneyland opened in California, Walt would walk around the park, personally testing all the rides, noticing if anything was out of place and asking the guests their opinions. If he saw something was wrong, he would make sure it was fixed.

Develop a high tolerance for risk

In 1955, Disneyland was the biggest gamble in the history of American business. Nothing like it had ever been attempted, so the general consensus was that it was an impossible undertaking. If Disneyland had failed, it would have bankrupted the company, but Walt had a vision and pushed forward anyway. Today, Disney theme parks bring in billions of dollars and attract millions of visitors each year.

Change your attitude towards failure

Walt Disney failed – a lot. One notable failure that ultimately spurred him to future success was losing the rights to one of his early creations, a little animated rabbit named Oswald. He also lost his equipment, his animators and his studio. It would have been very easy for Disney to give up at that point, but instead the man took what he'd learned from that immense misstep and came up with one of the most beloved characters ever created. On the train home from learning he'd lost Oswald, Walt sparked the idea for Mickey Mouse.

Believe in yourself, even if no one else does

Disney World in Florida opened five years after Walt's death. On opening day someone remarked to creative director Mike Vance that it was too bad Walt Disney hadn't lived to see it happen.

"He did see it, though," Vance replied. "And that's why it's here."

Throughout his career, Walt was repeatedly told what couldn't be done. He was told no one would sit through an animated feature film. He was told you couldn't mix animation and real-life actors. He was told his idea for a theme park would fail miserably. Time after time, he was told that his vision was impossible, yet despite all that, he had an unshakable belief in himself and what he was doing; in the end, that was all that mattered.

"It's kind of fun to do the impossible."
– Walt Disney

Reading for Success

I've learned a lot over the years from inspirational leaders such as Walt Disney and I continue to seek out more wisdom through the books I read. Personally, I make a point to read at least one book per week and that adds up to more than 50 a year.

Let's be clear: I'm not talking about browsing, skimming or speed reading. Good books deserve to be read slowly, deliberately and repeatedly. Between reading sessions, spend some time thinking about how these ideas relate to your situation. Remember, new thoughts and ideas are of no use if you do not apply them in your life. Many people will read an enlightening book or attend a motivating seminar that inflates them with confidence and direction only to have the glow wear off after a few days because they don't follow through. That's why it is so important to read, reread and apply.

Think of it this way: Ideas are the tools you will use to build the life you dream about. Once you have acquired some good tools, make a commitment to yourself to use them regularly. With application comes a deeper sense of understanding that will lead you to success sooner.

In his book *How to Study*, Arthur Kornhauser, an associate professor of business psychology at the University of Chicago, wrote: "Knowledge is acquired only through thinking and doing . . . learning is an active process. Use your knowledge by thinking, talking and writing about the things you are learning."

Next to following through, one of the biggest mistakes people make in regards to reading is putting a book down when they come across an idea they don't agree with. No one says that each point made will apply to you or that you have to agree with the author at every turn! Many of the best articles and books about success have been written for a sales or business audience; that doesn't mean that just because you are not involved in running a business you should ignore them. These books often contain principles and techniques that can be applied to many aspects of life. Be willing to explore other ways of thinking and take what you can from each work.

Here are some more tips on making the most of reading:

Coffee talk
Discuss and share ideas with others. Talk about what you've learned with friends and family. Even if you end up in the odd debate, you will be using what you learn.

Build your own library
Collect books, podcasts and articles that inspire you and review them whenever you need a little motivation in your life.

Share the wealth . . . and the wisdom
Send articles to friends and business associates. When you find topical information you think might help someone else, don't hesitate to pass it along. We could all use a little boost and a few fresh ideas now and then.

Thirty minutes a day could change your life
Read something useful, challenging or educational every day.

Thirty minutes spent with a book that motivates, excites and educates you will make a world of difference. My Speakers Roundtable colleague Charlie "Tremendous" Jones said, "We will be the same person in five years except for the people we meet, the places we go and the books we read." He also challenged me with the question, "What books are you rereading?"

The world according to . . . you
Keep a journal for your thoughts and ideas and try to carry it with you (whether it's in an actual book or a file stored on your device). This will help track your progress and make your learning more tangible. A journal is also a good place to record quotes that inspire you and list books you want to read.

Take it on the road
Listen to educational, motivational and inspirational recordings (or podcasts) while you commute. Forget the bad-news stations and talk radio. Fill your mind with the best information you can find and you will arrive at your destination feeling energized.

It has often been said, "Success is a journey, not a destination." It's still true. Associate reading and learning with having fun, growing as an individual and getting closer to achieving your dreams; reading should be enjoyable as well as educational.

"Learning lessons is a little like reaching maturity.
You're not suddenly more happy, wealthy
or powerful, but you understand the world around you
better, and you're at peace with yourself.
Learning life's lessons is not about making your life perfect,
but about seeing life as it was meant to be."
– Elisabeth Kübler-Ross

CHAPTER 27

YOUR STORY IS YOUR CALLING CARD

"Success is waiting for every one of us as long as we are
willing to be moulded by our particular circumstances. Success
is not something you ever have to chase; it's something
you only need to learn to expect and accept."
– Sol Hicks

T here's a Chinese proverb that states, "A single conversation with a wise person is better than 10 years of study."

I met such a wise person in an unusual way. Here's the story:

First off, what do you think the odds are of two 75-year-old men (an American from Atlanta, Georgia, and a Canadian from Vancouver, British Columbia) being in Barcelona, Spain, on the same day?

OK, not an earth-shattering coincidence, but wait, there's more.

What if these two men were both internationally known professional speakers?

And what if these same two 75-year-old men were travelling with their wives, both couples married for 50 years, and both staying on the same deck?

What if I also told you that these two fellows were travelling on the same two cruises back-to-back from Barcelona to Venice and would find themselves in side-by-side cabins for the duration of their voyage?

I think now you'll agree: the chances are pretty slim!

The 40,700-tonne Silversea cruise liner we were on was called the *Silver Muse*. Manfrédi Lefebvre d'Ovidio, former chairman of Silversea Cruises, once said: "Travelling the world is relatively easy nowadays, but to do it in superlative luxury? This can only be done with Silversea."

I echo his sentiment. What a unique opportunity it was to meet my cabin neighbour, Solomon Hicks, aboard one of Silversea's luxury cruises.

The story of how I met Solomon is just as unusual and just as unlikely as the two of us being on the same cruise to begin with. It was day two of our voyage and the ship was docked in Monte Carlo. The weather was simply glorious so my wife Kay decided to go explore the shops in town. I, on the other hand, saw the opportunity to enjoy some rest and relaxation, and instead decided to kick back on our cabin deck in my shorts and T-shirt with a book in hand.

Sitting in my lounge chair, I looked out at the sea as I digested what I had just been reading and it was at that moment I heard the door of the cabin next to me slide open. My neighbour had also stepped out onto his deck. With privacy walls between each suite, he must have assumed he was alone (just as I had), because he started to read something aloud. At first I thought perhaps it was a letter to a friend that he was composing. However, as he went on it started to sound more like a businessman making a pitch. He spoke very confidently.

A few minutes into his presentation, it occurred to me this wasn't a letter or a proposal to a client – he was rehearsing a speech! As a speaker myself, I recognized how he was trying the same line a few different ways for effect and to smooth out the structure of his presentation. And he was good – so much so that I put down my book and gave him my rapt attention for the rest of his 35-minute rehearsal.

As soon as Solomon was done, I leapt to my feet and gave him a hearty round of applause! He was stunned; he thought all the guests had gone ashore. I apologized for eavesdropping and told him how riveting and impactful his speech was, and since he was just next door, I asked if I could come over and shake his hand.

> "Your story is your calling card," says Sol. "People who get to know your story connect with you and your journey."

Five seconds later, we were exchanging business cards and

making plans to get together with our wives for dinner that evening. As it turned out, Solomon was rehearsing a speech he was slated to give later that month at the Million Dollar Roundtable convention. The Million Dollar Roundtable, of which Sol is a member, is a trade association formed in 1927 that represents the world's best sales professionals in the life-insurance-based, financial services industry.

As an insurance salesman, Sol has 12 No. 1 trophies to his credit. Seven of them were earned during his more than 35 years with Prudential Financial and he is one of only two agents in Prudential's 130-plus-year history to finish No. 1 seven times. Sol is also the author of three books. *Wise Guys Finish First* is an autobiographical portrait of overcoming incredible obstacles to get to the top; in *The Secret Life of a #1 Salesman*, he shares the mindset, values and daily disciplines that led him to his great success; *Making Disciples* is his latest book, which reveals the secret to creating a loyal client base devoted to helping build your business.

After a few more dinners and the odd drink, we parted company with Sol and his wife Carol in Venice with the promise to stay in touch and exchange some of our books.

Two old speakers meeting on what we both thought was a semi-deserted cruise ship in the middle of the Mediterranean – what are the odds of that?

So what did I learn from the very dynamic Solomon Hicks?

On his very first date with Carol, he asked her to marry him!

HAVE COURAGE! TAKE A CHANCE!

But she said "No."

That didn't deter him, and for the next 85 days he proceeded to ask her the same question each day until finally she said yes. PERSISTENCE!

They married just four days after she accepted and 55 years later they are still together and still very much in love.

Solomon asks, "Who's telling you you're not good enough? You're not talented enough?" YOU ARE! "That you're not smart enough? You're not good-looking enough?" YOU ARE! We must stop this thinking and realize that, in the end, we become what we think we are. "The best thing you have to offer the world is YOU."

At the end of each presentation Solomon gives, he tells the audience to remember these numbers:

10-10-80-72

10 – give 10 per cent of your income to charity

10 – save 10 per cent of your income (to plan for your future)

80 – live on 80 per cent of your income (enjoy the fruits of your labour)

72 – the rule of 72 says your money doubles every 7.2 years (if you do the math based on the rate of interest your money is presently earning, your calculation will help decide whether you want to be more aggressive with your savings and investments)

Getting to know Solomon Hicks was quite the experience. One of Sol's favourite expressions is the foundation for his success as a sought-after international speaker. "Your story is your calling card," says Sol. "People who get to know your story connect with you and your journey. They have similar stories and maybe haven't even realized how those experiences impacted their life and maybe even changed their destiny. So, what's your story?"

Here are just a few more life lessons I gleaned from Sol's books:

- Don't wait for your life to become amazing – make it so!
- People will forgive you for just about anything except lying to them.
- Your passion has to be greater than what you are paid. The fire in your belly has to burn hotter than your greatest fear.
- Commitment must come from us first. We must show ourselves to be trustworthy before we can ask a client to trust us.
- Bring more to the table than your appetite, have something of value to offer others.
- If you want to get out of the hole, don't study the hole.
- Today is new. Treat it that way. Make it into whatever you want it to be.
- As a coach and mentor to hundreds of people around the world, Sol is a strong proponent of the idea that a candle loses nothing when it lights another candle. In fact, it creates twice as much light.

CHAPTER 28

PETER'S 12 PRINCIPLES FOR SUCCESSFUL (AND RICH) SALESPEOPLE

"Our greatest weakness lies in giving up. The most
certain way to succeed is always to try just one more time."
– Thomas Edison

1. Like it or not, the job that determines the success of your business, whether it fails or succeeds, is SALES. Therefore, your No. 1 job is to sell . . . period! No ifs, ands or buts! Everything in business starts with sales. Nothing happens until somebody sells something. N-O-T-H-I-N-G. From the moment you fire up your computer until you head home for the day, it's all about selling.
2. Find a mentor. Buy them lunch. Be prepared with questions. Ask for advice. Ask for success principles and take notes.

3. Read every day. Read a minimum of one book a week and it will change your life! If you're not reading, how are you growing? (FYI, billionaire Warren Buffett reads six to seven hours daily.)

4. Set goals, not wishes. Write them down where you can read them every day.
   1. Sales volume.
   2. Number of calls.
   3. Number of sales.

   At the end of every day, review your numbers to gauge your success (the numbers never lie) and then set your goals for the next day.

5. Live on 80 per cent of your income, invest the rest for your future. Preparing for your future starts today! Not tomorrow, not next week, not next year.

6. Learn to listen more and talk less. Take notes. Most people never listen. Ask people better questions. Make eye contact.

7. Avoid lunches with your fellow salespeople unless you are actually solving a specific sales problem. Eat at your desk; get some exercise – walk around the block.

8. Say to yourself, "Do it now" and repeat it often.

9. Do more for your customer than they expect. Go beyond the norm. It's not about you, it's about them and the product and the service. It's much easier to keep an existing customer happy than it is to find a new one.

10. Don't give up! Give it your all every day. Run it like your own business.

11. If the customer says no, ask why. Then come back with: "If I could eliminate that, would you commit?" If they still say no, there's something else at play – find out what that is.

– And finally –

12. SMILE! Say "please" and "thank you" and treat everyone you meet as a potential customer. Remember to ask, "What can I do for you?" "What are you trying to do?" "How can I help with that?" Then follow up and follow through.

CHAPTER 29

HACK YOUR LIFE

"Today you are you, that is truer than true.
There is no one alive who is youer than you."
– Dr. Seuss

I n his book *Authentic Happiness*, Dr. Martin Seligman notes, "You cannot be anything you want to be – but you can be a lot more of who you already are."

Too many of us try too hard to be something we're not, or worse yet, we devote more time to fixing our shortcomings than developing our strengths. Sometimes we do it to please others, sometimes we do it because we think it will lead to wealth, fame or success. More often, it ends in depression, failure and disappointment.

Each of us is valuable because of our particular talents, so why focus on what we're not?

Almost 20 years ago, Donald O. Clifton and the Gallup Organization (the global research company famous for the Gallup poll) developed a tool called the Strengths Finder to help people discover and develop their natural talents. Drawing on more than 40 years of research, they discovered the following basic truths about human achievement and success:

- A life spent focusing on improving our weaknesses leads to dissatisfaction and mediocrity.
- Spending time doing what we love and are best at is what drives success.
- We cannot be great at everything, so we need to acknowledge our limitations, build on our strengths and get on with life.
- Every day should be spent focusing on developing what we believe to be our true gifts.
- When choosing who to work with, opposing strengths can lead to the strongest partnerships.

> *"Very few people do this anymore. It's too risky.*
> *First of all, it's a hell of a responsibility to be yourself.*
> *It's much easier to be somebody else or nobody at all."*
> – Sylvia Plath

Blogger Chris Guillebeau talks about how his choice to become a "travel hacker" (someone who travels the world without spending much money) meant that he had to make choices about what's important to him. Before he was 35 years old, Chris visited every country in the world. To achieve his dream, he chose not to have a car or a house; instead he took transit or rode his bike and he rented an apartment so that he could dedicate his money to adventures. He also doesn't have a "job"; instead he earns income from products and services offered through his website and blog, "The Art of Non-Conformity."

> The truth is that beyond basic food, shelter and transportation, everything else that we choose to spend our money on is exactly that, a choice – our choice.

When Chris (who calls Portland, Oregon, home) travels, the people he meets are always fascinated by his lifestyle and invariably say something like, "That sounds amazing, I wish I could do that."

"What's keeping you from it?" is his standard response.

It's an excellent question and one that we should all ask when we find ourselves making rationalizations for why we aren't living our dreams.

"You don't have to live your life the way other people expect, there is usually more than one way to accomplish something," says Chris, who added the title *New York Times* bestselling author to his list of accomplishments with the publication of his book *The $100 Startup*. (His most recent book is called *Side Hustle.*) "If you don't decide for yourself what you want to get out of life, someone else will end up deciding for you," he says.

Perhaps the most common rationalization for not taking action is a familiar one: "I don't have the money to pursue my dream." But chances are, if you live in North America you have more than enough money to meet your basic needs and plenty left over for the things that you want, such as your house or condo (complete with a big mortgage payment), a car (or two or three), a smartphone, Netflix and high-speed internet service, just to name a few recurring expenses that can add up very quickly.

The truth is that beyond basic food, shelter and transportation, everything else that we choose to spend our money on is exactly that, a choice – our choice. We choose what we value when we decide how to spend our time, money and other resources.

Are you willing to sacrifice your dreams in order to live the life you have or will you instead sacrifice a few comforts and do what it takes to realize your dream?

Here are two questions that Chris suggests people ask themselves to help determine if they are on the right path to fulfilling their dreams:

Am I satisfied with my job and career?

Your job should do more than simply provide income for the rest of your life. Ask yourself, what am I working for? Am I working to make a living or to make a life? If your work supports your goals, that's great. If it doesn't, maybe it's time to change.

What are my financial priorities?

If you have difficulty answering, there's an easy way to tell.

Check your credit card statements and receipts for the past six months. Where you've been spending your money is where your priorities are. Once you fully understand what you want, it's usually not difficult to get it.

Chris's advice for dealing with critics and naysayers? "At all stages of life, people will gladly offer you unsolicited lists of things you 'must' do, be or have. Most of the time you can nod your head, walk away and ignore them."

The life you have is the one you've made for yourself. If you want something different, you're going to have to do something differently.

Many people struggle to find something they are truly passionate about. The philosopher Joseph Campbell once said, "If you follow your bliss, you put yourself on a kind of track that has been there all the while, waiting for you, and the life that you ought to be living is the one you are living. When you can see that, you begin to meet people who are in your field of bliss, and they open doors for you. I say, follow your bliss and don't be afraid, and doors will open where you didn't know they were going to be."

Unfortunately, many people have never experienced that feeling of being plugged into the world around them. Instead, they get up in the morning and go through the motions, feeling tired, frustrated and even resentful about the work they do every day.

William Bridges, author of *Managing Transitions*, says, "Nothing less than finding what you were meant to be and do will give you the motivation and the capability that today's work world demands. Identifying your life work is no longer an escapist fantasy. It is a condition of being successful."

So, let's get started. Small steps taken today can lead to big changes tomorrow. Here are five steps to get you on the way to finding your purpose:

1. Get a grip on your fear

We all know that fear has its place, but it shouldn't stand in the way of finding your purpose. In her book *Feel the Fear and Do It Anyway*, Dr. Susan Jeffers says, "The fear will never go away as long as you continue to grow. Every time you take a step into the unknown, you experience fear. There is no point in saying, 'When I am no longer afraid, then I will do it.' You'll be waiting for a long time. The fear is part of the package." Just know that with each little step you take into unknown territory, a pattern of strength develops.

"You begin feeling stronger and stronger and stronger," explains Dr. Jeffers. "As you face your fears, you will become more and more aware that you can truly handle anything that life hands you."

2. Get real

You've seen the ads for easy-money jobs: "Earn $1,000 a week clicking ads on the Internet from the comfort of your own home." Sounds great, right? Well, as Joe Segal often says, "There's no free lunch, even when someone else is buying."

So snap out of it! Finding your purpose, like everything else worthwhile, takes time and effort. A good place to start is by acknowledging the good things you already have in your life, the talents and skills you possess – then look for ways you can build on those strengths.

3. Get involved

You have probably racked your brain trying to figure out what your ideal career is. But quite possibly, you've never even heard of the type of work that would be a perfect fit for you. In fact, many people who follow their passions find that it leads them into uncharted territory and eventually they "invent" a career that is custom-fit to them. Let your natural curiosity guide you and look for ideas in the "world" of your interests. Make it a point to simply do things you like, without trying so hard to figure out how they could turn into a career. This process will also bring you in contact with others who share your passion.

4. Get focused

Instead of focusing on what you *don't* want – meaningless work, office politics, someone else calling the shots – zoom in on the life you *do* want. Five minutes a day spent visualizing your ideal work life and fashioning a plan to get there will move you far closer to your goal than 30 minutes of complaining.

5. Get a new perspective

Family aside, nobody knows you better than your friends

and close associates. Put together a questionnaire and send it out via email to at least 10 people you know. You can pose such questions as:

- What do you think I am good at?
- Do you notice any natural talents in me that you think I could develop into a career?
- How am I getting in my own way when it comes to the ideal job search?

Within a few days, you should have enough feedback to discover some trends – for example, you may notice the majority of your friends think you would be a great event organizer, even if you take your planning skills for granted – and at the very least, you will have some objective ideas about your strengths and any behaviour that may be holding you back.

"Nothing is really work unless you would
rather be doing something else."
– J.M. Barrie

CHAPTER 30

THE "NOT TO DO" LIST

"The secret of a person's success is determined
by what he or she does daily."
– John Maxwell

S hortly after my 20th book, *The Power of Tenacity,* was published, I received plenty of tips on other, similar books I should read.

At the top of the list was Angela Duckworth's *Grit – The Power of Passion*, which I tracked down in the psychology section of a Barnes & Noble.

We all have dreams and goals, or at least we should.

In her book, Duckworth tells a story about self-made billionaire Warren Buffett and his longtime pilot. That story offers an important lesson about what separates extraordinarily successful people from everyone else.

Mike Flint was Buffett's personal airplane pilot for 10 years. Flint had flown for four different U.S. presidents prior to that, so he'd had a pretty good career, yet still felt as though he hadn't achieved all he wanted to.

So one day Buffett jokingly said to Flint, "The fact that you're still working for me tells me I'm not doing my job. You should be out going after more of your goals and dreams."

When Flint asked Buffett for advice on how he might go about doing that, Buffett offered a simple three-step process for prioritizing what to focus on.

First, he instructed Flint to write down his 25 top goals and then circle the top five most important ones.

Making the list of 25 was easy, but choosing five to prioritize was much more difficult since everything on the list was important (after all, that's why he wrote them down). But Buffett insisted that he could only pick five, so after some time and thought, he made five circles.

> Instead of making endless lists of the things you need to do, ask yourself: "What is the most important thing I can do today, the one thing that would make everything else in my life either easier or unnecessary?"

"Are you sure these are the absolute highest priority for you?" Buffet asked.

Flint confidently replied that they were.

"Then, separate the top five into their own list and goals 6-25 get put on a 'Not to Do' list."

Why create a "Not to Do" list?

Shifting our time and focus between too many priorities is the reason many of us end up with 25 half-finished projects instead of five completed ones. The trick is to ignore everything on the "Not to Do" list until you've achieved your top five goals.

Buffett's approach turns our traditional understanding of what it takes to be successful on its head, but his results speak for themselves. It also challenges the theory that multitasking and the drive to achieve as much as possible is the path to success.

So instead of making endless lists of the things you need to do, ask yourself: "What is the most important thing I can do today, the one thing that would make everything else in my life either easier or unnecessary?"

It couldn't be simpler than that.

Warren Buffett is the third-richest man in the world. He's also considered to be the greatest investor to have ever lived. What's funny is that Buffett has achieved all of his success not by doing more than his peers . . . but by doing *less*!

Seriously.

For example, did you know that Warren Buffett:

1. Doesn't have a computer in his office.
2. Spends most of the day reading up on subjects that are important to him.
3. Keeps a calendar that is nearly empty.
4. Prefers to seize a few big opportunities when they come along instead of chasing after many.

5. Delegates tasks/projects almost to the point of abdication.

Warren Buffett's secret to success is intense focus. Instead of doing more, he does less – although doing less should not be confused with idleness. The man works incredibly hard, but he only works incredibly hard on things that are the most important to him.

Why is it, as time goes on, that many of us stop making goals? Is it an age thing? Age means nothing, just ask Warren Buffett, who recently turned 89, or my friend Joe Segal, who is 94. You don't want to be sitting on your deathbed saying, "If only . . ."

There are thousands to tell you it cannot be done,
There are thousands to prophesy failure;
There are thousands to point out to you one by one,
The dangers that wait to assail you.
But just buckle in with a bit of a grin,
Just take off your coat and go to it;
Just start in to sing as you tackle the thing
That "cannot be done," and you'll do it.
– Edgar Guest

CHAPTER 31

FAILURE IS AN EVENT, NOT A PERSON

I'm very blessed to have seven grandchildren: Benjamin, Cate, London, Sofie, Carys, Grayson and Oscar. The eldest is 13 years old. The youngest is just two.

Kids are natural learners, we don't have to teach them how to do it. Watching them learn new skills like walking, talking and riding a bike, I've come to realize the many reasons why children pick things up so quickly: they don't care if they fail. They're not looking around to see who saw them make a mistake. They don't worry about looking foolish. Kids just want to master the skill, so they put everything they've got into it.

As adults, we should follow the example of children. Unfortunately, for most of us, when our endeavours don't turn out quite the way we expected, we become discouraged and lose all sense of perspective about our talent and potential. Remember this, though: in the fullness of time, 70 per cent of your decisions will be wrong. I know it sounds a little grim, but that's actually a pretty good average – in baseball, if you walk up to the plate and fail to get on-base 70 per cent of the time, they call you a hero. So you must be willing to keep trying, and risk striking out, in order to reach your goals.

> *"Would you like me to give you a formula for success?*
> *It's quite simple, really: Double your rate of failure.*
> *You are thinking of failure as the enemy of success. But it*
> *isn't at all. You can be discouraged by failure*
> *or you can learn from it, so go ahead and make mistakes.*
> *Make all you can. Because remember, that's where*
> *you will find success."*
> – Thomas J. Watson

Most of us view failure as a bad thing, but is it really? Being wrong teaches us to be creative. If you're never willing to be wrong, then you'll never be forced to innovate. You'll just repeat what you already know over and over. Real life comes with ups and downs, successes and failures – by experimenting to find what works, we learn valuable lessons from each one of our mistakes, lessons that we can apply to other areas of our lives. Einstein knew that there is no such thing as successful experimentation without failure, children know it instinctively, and now you know it too.

Important Things We Can Learn From Our Failures

1. Failure teaches us to be flexible and make corrections when things aren't working the way we planned.

During the 1940s, one young man chose to skip university in order to pursue his dream of becoming the next Benny Goodman. Going against his parents' advice, he began playing in a jazz band.

Unfortunately, his musical abilities weren't prodigious enough to pay the bills and he soon realized he was just another musician teetering on the brink of unemployment. However, unlike many of his fellow musicians, he was very good at managing what money he had, which meant that those periods of unemployment weren't nearly as devastating for him as they were for others.

Recognizing his talent for money management, his musician colleagues began to pay him to manage their finances as well. This led the young man to rethink his career goals and it also changed the course of his life.

That young man's name was Alan Greenspan and he went on to serve as longtime chairman of the United States Federal Reserve (1987-2006). His failure as a musician not only taught him resilience and self-reliance (important skills that we can all use in life), it also taught him that he had other, significant talents to share with the world. Just like Mr. Greenspan, our failures can help us to discover how our interests and aptitudes might lead us to our true purpose.

Sometimes, finding out what doesn't work is as important

as finding out what does. When we fail, we eliminate at least one of the possibilities on our list and are free to pursue other ideas and options. In many ways, failure can actually be very cleansing. It gives us the ability to start anew with a modified or entirely new direction that has a new opportunity (and probability) for success. The moment we move on, we have a fresh chance to succeed (or fail again) and the opportunity to apply what we have learned.

Of course, nobody likes to miss the mark, but there is so much we can learn from each attempt, and every time we try again it gets easier. Imagine Thomas Edison in his workshop, trying to develop the light bulb. It took him 9,000 tries before he finally made one that worked. But with every attempt, he made corrections that helped him to improve, and in doing so he pushed himself that little bit closer to success. Like Edison, if we stay flexible and keep trying, we can literally fail our way to success.

2. Failure teaches us that we are never too smart to make a mistake.

Albert Einstein was clearly a brilliant man whose work contributed much to the advancement of science and our understanding of physics. But if you think that geniuses get it right every time, you'd be wrong. Einstein made plenty of mistakes, famous ones even, but that never stopped him from continuing to develop new theories about the universe.

In the book *Einstein's Mistakes: The Human Failings of Genius*, author Hans C. Ohanian talks about how scientists have identified serious flaws in four of the five papers that established Einstein's reputation in theoretical physics back in 1905. Ohanian also points out Einstein's repeated failure to provide valid proof for his most famous equation: $E = mc2$ and talks about how, despite his repeated mistakes and in some cases, because of them, time after time Einstein achieved theoretical breakthroughs that eluded other scientists – which goes a long way to explain why he remains an icon so many decades later.

Imagine if Einstein believed that his genius meant that he wasn't allowed to make mistakes, or worse, allowed his failures to stop him from continuing with the development of his theories. Like Einstein, we should allow our failures to act as stepping stones.

3. Failure teaches us that we can't always get what we want, but sometimes not getting what we want leads us to discover something even better.

Following World War II, Soichiro Honda applied for the position of engineer with the Toyota Motor Corporation but was turned down. Unemployed, he started to produce homemade scooters in his own small workshop and sell them to friends and neighbours. As word spread and demand for his economical scooters grew, he decided to take the plunge and start his own company: Honda. Since then, that company has grown to become the world's largest motorcycle manufacturer and one of the most profitable automakers – beating giants such as General Motors and Chrysler. With a global network of 437 subsidiaries, today Honda develops, manufactures and markets a wide variety of products ranging from small general-purpose engines and scooters to specialty sports cars.

4. Failure teaches us that we can survive a lot more than we imagine.

Failure is something to celebrate because it means that we have actually made an attempt at accomplishing something significant, we've stretched beyond our comfort zone and lived to tell about it. It builds our resilience and in realizing that we can survive a failure, we are more confident about pushing our own boundaries even further.

I remember my very first business failure. Like many entrepreneurs, I dreamed of being my own boss, calling the shots and ultimately building a hugely successful enterprise. But we all have to start somewhere and I began with a concession stand at the Pacific National Exhibition (PNE) – which is a large, 17-day-long end-of-summer fair that takes place in Vancouver each year. Back then, I had a full-time job at *The Columbian* newspaper in New Westminster selling advertising but wanted to buy a second family car so my wife could have her own transportation while I was at work. Unfortunately, on my salary, a car for Kay seemed many years away.

Enter the business opportunity; some associates of mine were selling a concession stand that they had run at the PNE the previous year. It was called Bunny's Foot Long Hot Dogs and from the financials they provided, it looked like it had made a nice profit. It also appeared to be a quick and easy venture that would allow me to get my feet wet running my own business and bring in the cash for a second car.

For a modest amount, I purchased the hot dog stand – and that's when my troubles began. Suddenly, I was bombarded with problems I hadn't even begun to think about. For example, I had no idea who was going to manage the enterprise. I also didn't know where to order supplies or how much it would cost for stock. In addition, I would have to find staff to run the stand morning to night for the 17 days of the fair, not to mention contract negotiations with the fair itself over their cut of the profits.

> In the same way that sadness can teach us to savour the happy moments, failure provides us with something to measure our successes against.

We eventually decided that my wife would be the one to run it, and I know you probably saw this coming, but at the time, with visions of easy money in my head, I didn't; that created the biggest problem of all: how was my wife going to get to work? She didn't have a car!

There was no way around it, we would have to buy a car before we had sold even one hot dog; so much for planning ahead. We settled on an Austin 1100, which cost around $475 – a great deal of money. The kicker was that we had to pay cash because we hadn't yet established a good credit rating.

In the end, my mom, dad and I all worked alongside Kay for 17 days straight from 10 a.m. to midnight. We also couldn't afford a babysitter, so Kay brought our young daughter Samantha with her every day to work.

I think Samantha must have eaten whatever profits there were that summer (we found out she really loves hot dogs). When the 17 days were over and the smell of grilled meat had finally been washed off of our clothes, we barely broke even due to the fact that it rained every single day of the fair. Exhausted and happy that Kay at least had her car now, I happily returned to my job at the paper . . . at least until the next entrepreneurial idea hit.

Now, a lot of people might come away from that experience thinking, "Wow, I'm not very good at this whole business thing: the planning, the organization, the budgeting and the management, never mind dealing with all of the elements that are beyond my control like the weather and how many customers show up." Not me. I learned so many valuable lessons from that summer selling hot dogs in the rain. Perhaps the most important thing: we should never be afraid to try a new venture. Because the only way to develop the skills necessary to run a business is by actually doing it. Just like everything else in life, we learn by doing.

Of course, it is inevitable that we will make mistakes along the way, but hopefully we will also learn some valuable lessons and our mistakes will make us stronger, wiser and more confident that we can survive anything, even failure.

5. Failure teaches us to appreciate our successes.

In the same way that sadness can teach us to savour the happy moments, failure provides us with something to measure our successes against. As humans, we are designed to appreciate contrast. If we have too much of one thing, we want something else. If things are going along too smoothly, we'll do something to shake them up and make life more interesting. We like to have challenges, something to work towards and the sense of accomplishment that comes with conquering a difficult task. With each failure, we become more determined than ever to succeed and our eventual success is made all the more sweet for our struggle.

6. Failure teaches us perseverance.

Here is a quote from NBA legend Michael Jordan: "I've missed more than 9,000 shots in my career. I've lost almost 300 games. 26 times, I've been trusted to take the game-winning shot and missed. I've failed over and over and over again in my life. And that is why I succeed."

One of the greatest gifts of failure is the knowledge that failure is never final, unless we choose to give up.

At the age of eight, Nick Vujicic decided that he wanted to end his life. Born without arms or legs, unable to do many of the things that we all take for granted, he realized that he would not have a normal life – with a job, a wife and family – and believed that he would also never be able to contribute to his community in a meaningful way. Nick decided to drown himself in the bathtub, but when it came down to the moment of truth, he couldn't do it. He thought about his parents and all of the love and support they had given him and also the guilt it would place on them if he killed himself.

Instead of giving up, which would have been quite understandable, Nick decided that there must be some other purpose for him and he set about discovering what that purpose could be. One day, after hearing the inspiring story of another man with severe disabilities, Nick realized he had a great deal to share with the world – the story of his struggles, his triumphs (he enjoys boating, swimming, diving, fishing and golf), his incredible sense of humour and his inspirational message.

Today, he visits schools and talks to children of all ages about being thankful for what you do have, not bitter about what you don't. It is especially touching to see the impact he has on teen audiences when he jokes around with them, demonstrates his many abilities and speaks to their biggest fears.

Discovering that we can turn our lives around, choose a different path or embrace a new idea at any age, in any set of circumstances, is liberating and can motivate us to seek the wisdom of others who have had different experiences, and can provide the momentum that will propel us to successes beyond our imaginings.

Canadian artist and icon Emily Carr painted for years without critical success. In her early 40s, she decided to give up art and return to her hometown of Victoria to run a rooming house and breed dogs. For 15 years, she painted very little. Lucky for the rest of us, she met Lawren Harris of the Group of Seven, who encouraged her to renew her interest in painting. As a result, Carr produced the work for which she is best known after the age of 57 and went on to see her art recognized for its "stunning originality and strength" and have it exhibited across Canada and in London, Paris, Washington and Amsterdam.

Sometimes, you might need to change direction but you can't quit.

7. Failure teaches us to differentiate between what is important and what is not so important in our lives.

That's exactly what happened with author J.K. Rowling, leading her to finally sit down and write the *Harry Potter* series, which subsequently turned her into a billionaire. In a moving speech she gave at Harvard on the topic of failure, Rowling described in her own words how hitting rock bottom, being unemployed and living on social assistance finally helped her fulfill her dream of being an author.

"So why do I talk about the benefits of failure?" she asked her audience. "Simply because failure meant a stripping away of the inessential. I stopped pretending to myself that I was anything other than what I was, and began to direct all my energy into finishing the only work that mattered to me. Had I really succeeded at anything else, I might never have found the determination to succeed in the one arena I believed I truly belonged. I was set free, because my greatest fear had already been realized, and I was still alive, and I still had a daughter whom I adored, and I had an old typewriter and a big idea. And so rock bottom became the solid foundation on which I rebuilt my life."

Failure has a way of focusing our attention like nothing else because we learn very quickly by experiencing it what our priorities are. We learn what we can and can't live without, we discover our strengths, our weaknesses and our greatest desires. Essentially, our failures highlight our values and help us to define what is important in our lives. For example, the person who puts their family before all else and really works at building a successful home life will probably not have a high-powered career, but will certainly have a close and nurturing relationship with their spouse and children. Likewise, the individual who thrives on building their career and putting in 80 or more hours a week will undoubtedly experience professional success, but surely their closest relationships will suffer as a result. Like the saying goes, "It is possible to have everything we want in life, just not all at the same time." Therefore, we can use our failures to help pinpoint and define what is most important so we can focus our time, energy and effort on that area and let the rest fall to the sidelines.

Something to Think About

"Failure is, in a sense, the highway to success . . ."
– John Keats

"I have learned throughout my life as a composer
chiefly through my mistakes and pursuits of false assumptions,
not by my exposure to founts of wisdom and knowledge."
– Igor Stravinsky

Fear of making mistakes is one of the biggest obstacles to having an interesting and fulfilling life. If you aren't making any mistakes, chances are you're not trying very hard at whatever you are doing. Successful people make lots of errors and they learn valuable lessons as a result. The expectation that things need to go perfectly is unrealistic and extremely limiting. Not only are mistakes a wonderful source of insight that we can use to make progress towards achieving our dreams, at times they are absolutely necessary to make us stop and pay attention. Sometimes we have to hit that brick wall to realize we need to try a different tack.

So next time you make a mistake, don't beat yourself up. Instead, be thankful for the insight you've been given and ask yourself, "How can I apply what I've learned?" No mistake should ever go to waste.

Change Your Attitude Towards Failure

Why are you afraid of failure? Most people fear failure for one of two reasons. Either they believe that failure makes them a bad person that others look down on, or they are afraid that they will lose all their wealth and material possessions if they fail. Both of these are misconceptions.

Failure isn't a person, it's an event. When you fail, you are not a failure. A failure, even a significant one, doesn't magically wipe out all of your successes. Will others look down on you if you fail? Some people might, but you can't control the thoughts of other people – so why worry about them?

As for losing all your money, there are much more devastating things that could happen, like losing a loved one or your own health. Failure can be uncomfortable and unpleasant, but it is not life-threatening. Nothing great is ever accomplished without the ever-present possibility of failure and since we will never be able to outrun our fears, the best thing to do is face up to them. When we do, more often than not, we realize they are not half as terrible as we imagined them to be.

So, put your doubts aside and go for it, because the only true failure happens when you cease to try. Even when things don't work out as you expected, don't take it personally. Dust yourself off and move on. Learn from your mistakes and remember that failure always offers an opportunity of one kind or another – an opportunity to stretch beyond our usual boundaries, to learn something valuable or to make previously undreamt-of connections. Remembering this positive face of failure and focusing on it will go a long way towards changing your attitude about it. Once you accept that failure can actually be good for you, you're well on your way to a happier, more fulfilling life.

Let Yourself – and Others – Make Mistakes

Social psychologist Heidi Grant Halvorson has an interesting take on mistakes. According to her research, people who give themselves "permission to screw up," actually make fewer mistakes and master new skills faster. The reason is that they take a "get better" approach to goals rather than a "be good" approach.

Here's how it works.

When we have a "be good" mindset, we put a lot of pressure on ourselves to perform well and this can create a lot of anxiety, particularly when it is a task we haven't performed many times before. Nothing interferes with performance quite like anxiety and that makes us much more prone to mistakes and, ultimately, failure.

However, when we tackle a goal with a "get better" approach, our focus turns away from our performance to learning and improving. As a result, we accept that it is OK to make some mistakes along the way, which allows us to stay motivated and focused on our goal despite any setbacks that occur.

Halvorson, who is the author of *Succeed: How We Can Reach Our Goals*, offers three helpful steps for reframing goals:

1. Start by embracing the fact that when something is difficult and unfamiliar, it will take time to really get a handle on it. You might make some mistakes and that's OK.

2. Remember to ask for help when you run into trouble. Needing help doesn't mean you aren't capable – in fact, the opposite is true. Only the very foolish believe they can do everything on their own.

3. Don't compare yourself to others. Instead, compare your performance today to your performance yesterday; getting better is about progress, not perfection.

When you give yourself permission to make mistakes, your focus shifts from you to your goal, which is where it should be.

Something else I learned from Joe Segal: Don't get caught up in trying to achieve perfection. "Ultimately, it is persistence that will pay off, so forget about perfection," says Joe. "There really isn't enough time in the world for us to worry about getting it right all the time. Besides, perfection isn't about doing a good job, it is about being in control and it feeds an overbearing need to be right. It is a far better thing to be persistent, find a goal that captures your imagination and strive to achieve it."

As a leader, it is important for those you are leading to know it's OK for them to make mistakes as well. By modelling and coaching this behaviour, you give others within your organization permission to make mistakes and grow.

*"If you start thinking that only your biggest
and shiniest moments count, you're setting yourself up
to feel like a failure most of the time."*
– Col. Chris Hadfield

CHAPTER 32

THE NIGHT I INTERVENED ON BRIAN'S BEHALF

"Mothers all want their sons to grow up
to be president but they don't want them to become
politicians in the process."
– John F. Kennedy

A number of years ago, Canada Wide Media Ltd. entered into a contract with Quebecor, a huge media company headquartered in Montreal. At the time, they were the largest magazine printing company in Canada and former Prime Minister Brian Mulroney was chairman of their board of directors.

Bruce Wiesner was our account executive and Quebecor's head of operations in Western Canada. He has since moved on to the role of associate dean with the UBC Sauder School of

Business, which in 2017 named our Canada Wide Media Ltd. as Family Business of the Year. We were in some pretty heady company; past winners included Harry Rosen menswear, Shaw Communications, the McLean Group, Molson and Rogers Communications.

But I digress.

Transcontinental printing (which had contracts with Quebecor) had planned a North American dinner reception at the world-famous Plaza Hotel in New York for all the company's North American clients. And I was on the guest list.

Not one to turn down such an exciting opportunity to meet some of the really big publishers in North America, I packed my bags and headed to YVR for the non-stop direct flight to New York. Yes, I knew I was out of my league, but just being invited on the trip seemed to elevate my very small company in the eyes of fellow invitees.

Bruce had arranged for me to sit right next to Brian Mulroney, whom I had not met before, at the gala dinner. Brian couldn't have been more gracious, warm and friendly . . . he made me feel like a giant in this industry, even though he was well aware of my humble little operation.

The dinner and service at the Plaza were impeccable, with imported wine and magnificent food. Brian and I chatted during dinner until the very pretty waitress who was serving our table came by. Brian asked the waitress, "May I please have some more butter?"

"No," she replied.

"I'm sorry," said Brian, "Perhaps you misunderstand; may I please have some more butter?"

"No," came her response once more.

Wanting to be helpful, I jumped into action and said to the young woman, "Do you have any idea who you're talking to?"

"No," she said.

I pointed at Brian and said, "This is the Honourable Brian Mulroney, former prime minister of Canada. When he was prime minister, he was in charge of everything!"

"Well, do you know who I am?" asked the waitress.

"No," I said.

"I'm in charge of the butter!" she said.

We both laughed and Brian got his butter.

In 2007, a book titled *Memoirs* written by Brian was published and he sent me a personally signed copy and a note that read:

Pete:

With warmest congratulations on your great contributions to the industry and to Canada.

Best wishes,
Brian Mulroney

The signed book was a proud addition to my library.

Brian was elected Canada's 18th prime minister on September

4, 1984, and his victory was announced on national TV by the CBC. "I always said the CBC was an intelligent network," he quipped upon hearing the news.

Brian Mulroney is a man of great achievement, with much insight to offer. If you haven't read his book, add it to your list. It's a very personal account of a very significant period in Canadian history.

"A politician needs the ability to foretell
what is going to happen tomorrow, next week,
next month and next year. And to have the
ability afterwards to explain why it didn't happen."
– Winston Churchill

CHAPTER 33

LESSONS I LEARNED FROM JIMMY PATTISON

"One of the best ways to influence people
is to make them feel important."
– Roy T. Bennett

J immy Pattison was our first special guest at the *BCBusiness* Top 100 Luncheon back in 2011. He was the perfect choice, as Jimmy owned *BCBusiness* magazine before I bought it from him 30 years ago.

Shortly after his 90th birthday on October 1, 2018, Jimmy phoned to thank me for an email I had sent him a few weeks earlier wishing him well on his birthday. It was a simple gesture, one that some might liken to sending a thank-you note for receiving thank-you flowers. A bit unnecessary, but it's precisely this kind of gesture that endears him to me.

Jimmy first apologized that his phone call had come in later than he intended, as he'd just returned from a business trip to Asia. He has not slowed down – not even on his 90th birthday! In fact, just this summer Jimmy made a proposal to buy the outstanding stock of Canfor and take it private; currently, the Pattison Group owns 53 per cent of the company.

After thanking me for the birthday email, Jimmy tells me a bit about his trip and where he went.

Then he asks me, "How's business?"

All said, it was only a five-minute phone call, but he didn't have to phone at all.

Yet he did, and he took the time to ask me how I was doing. Nothing was rushed. I had his full attention. That's *class*.

If Jimmy Pattison, the richest person in British Columbia and the fifth-richest in all of Canada, can set aside five minutes in his day to make a phone call to acknowledge a gesture, to reconnect or to simply say hello, what extra measure could we be taking to maintain our business and personal relationships?

Every one of us is an influencer, whether we realize it or not; likewise, we are constantly being influenced by others. The big question for me and for you is, who do we influence and how do we influence them during our day-to-day interactions?

In 2017, Jimmy Pattison was presented with the Visionary Humanitarian Award at the David Foster Miracle Gala, which was held at Rogers Arena. It was the 30th anniversary of the gala and in keeping with the all-star theme of the event, Oprah Winfrey came to Vancouver to present Jimmy with the award.

As someone who started out from very humble beginnings and through sheer hard work and brilliance became one of the richest people in Canada, we could all learn a thing or two from Jimmy.

One of Oprah's telling comments was that whatever Jimmy commits to, he follows up and "it will be done."

It may not seem like a big thing, but ask yourself this: "How many people do I know who always keep their word?"

What I have learned as a result of my own long friendship with Jimmy is to expect that someone is always watching and being influenced by the example we set, therefore it is incumbent upon each of us to be a role model and a person of character.

When the man was asked if he had to start all over and build an empire in this day and age, would it be more difficult? "No, easier, because access to capital is much easier and there's much more change today than there used to be and it's rapid. Anytime there is change, there is opportunity," explained Jimmy. "I don't think I have ever seen more opportunity for young people than there is right now."

He continued: "I've had many people stop me on the street and say, 'You know, Jimmy, the best thing you ever did was fire me because I found something that suited me better.'"

"I think everybody's good at something, they just have to figure out what it is. Getting fired from something you're not good at gives you the opportunity and incentive to go find something better."

"Expect change. Analyze the landscape.
Take the opportunities. Stop being the chess piece;
become the player. It's your move."
– Tony Robbins

CHAPTER 34

THE PERSON WHO TAKES THE BEST NOTES, WINS!

"Great leaders are never
too proud to learn."
– John Donahoe

G reat leaders are listeners and they also take good notes. I learned this firsthand from Zig Ziglar, who was definitely one of a kind.

When the National Speakers Association held its annual conference in Washington, D.C., a number of years ago, it was my honour to be asked by the association's then-president Glenna Salsbury to present the keynote address at one of the luncheons. The invitation alone was a privilege to be sure (with a thousand other speakers in attendance), but the icing on the cake was news that one of the most respected and admired speakers in North

America – the famed Zig Ziglar, would be in the audience.

I can honestly say I never get nervous when I speak, but I can't say that's how I felt before this particular presentation knowing that Zig would be watching and listening!

So many thoughts ran through my head as I prepared:

What's my topic?

Do I have enough material?

Will it be relevant?

How's Zig going to respond?

It was a 30-minute keynote right after lunch and as I finished to a standing ovation from the audience, I thought to myself, "Not bad."

Just then, out of the corner of my eye, I saw Zig Ziglar coming towards me.

What would he say?

Did he like my speech?

Was he even listening to this random Canadian?

As he approached me, Zig put out his hand and said, "Fantastic job, Peter."

Then he went on to ask if I could clarify three of the points I'd spoken about. He even had a pad full of notes that he had taken during my remarks.

Zig Ziglar did in fact listen and he even asked questions.

I was very impressed and maybe that's why when I'm in meetings I always make sure to have my clipboard in front of me and I always write the letter "L" on the top left-hand corner to remind me to listen to whoever is presenting or speaking at a meeting.

One of Zig's most famous quotes is: "You can have everything in life you want, if you will just help other people get what they want."

Although he passed away a few years ago, Zig's message of inspiration, along with his many books and videos, still impact thousands of people today. Thanks to his son, Tom Ziglar, whom I have corresponded with a couple times, Zig's office, legacy and influence live on.

As mentioned, I always carry a notepad with me to every meeting, whether it's an internal staff meeting or a personal lunch with a client – because ideas, lessons and inspiration can come from all sorts of places.

Sometimes that inspiration can strike you rather inconveniently, at say 2 a.m. (which happens to me more often than I'd like . . . if only I could fall back to sleep after), so I think it's smart to keep a little notebook and pen handy at your bedside table during the night as well as carrying them during the day.

Need more inspiration to take good notes?

At McGill University in Montreal, students are not permitted to use laptops in their lecture halls. Professors argue that handwritten notes lead to better conceptual understanding than typed ones.

It turns out that handwriting notes is more effective for processing and retaining information than using an electronic device. Reviewing and even rewriting your notes is also beneficial because it gives you a chance to process critical information and identify any gaps in your knowledge. This type of note-taking and review can significantly improve your performance, as it trains your brain to process info in an effective and efficient way.

Indeed, according to *Forbes* magazine, note-taking can help you at all stages of your career. They recommend that you take notes any time there's a big change, whenever you're learning a new skill or any time you need to remember a large volume of information. Note-taking saves you from having to memorize everything you're learning and takes the pressure off of your overloaded brain, which allows you to better retain info. Notes also serve as a guide to help do your job better, because you can easily refer back to important info whenever you need to.

As a bonus, taking notes will make you smarter. When you have a pad filled with detailed, thoughtful notes (that you actually review from time to time), you start to discover links between things that you otherwise wouldn't have seen and have access to information that other people don't retain. This is how you'll come up with great ideas, form new connections and develop into the kind of innovator and leader who really makes things happen.

"If you aren't taking notes, you aren't learning."
– Ben Casnocha

CHAPTER 35

TOO MANY KISSES IN VENICE

"I love her, and that's the beginning
and end of everything."
– F. Scott Fitzgerald

J ust before Kay and I left for Europe to celebrate our 50th wedding anniversary, I met with my friend and Canada Wide Media client Pino Bacinello, who is the president and founder of Pacific M&A and Business Brokers Ltd. Pino gave me what I thought to be some very good travel advice for when Kay and I got to Venice – and he's Italian, so who was I to question him?

With a very serious face, Pino told me that it is tradition when travelling by gondola to kiss every time you pass under a bridge.

Well, I'm not sure if he was having me on or doing me a favour! What I can say is that on our gondola ride, Kay and I passed under several dozen bridges and I made good on Pino's alleged tradition each and every time.

Since returning home, we've learned the *real* tradition takes place under just a single bridge, the "Bridge of Sighs."

Venice, the city that conjures romance in the minds of all, was once the world's centre of commerce.

Some interesting facts I picked up:
- The history of Venice began in 400 A.D.
- Venice has 354 bridges (no, Kay and I did not cross over/ under each one).
- One of those bridges, the Liberty Bridge, is five kilometres long! It connects the centre of Venice with the Mestre district on the mainland.
- Another bridge, Ponte Maria Callas, was named after the famed opera singer Maria Callas. This bridge was created to allow easy access for patrons attending shows at La Fenice theatre, which is where Maria was "discovered" while performing.
- Because of the large number of tourists year-round, the cost of living in Venice is very high; very few Venetians can still afford to live in their own city.

We also got a lesson on the main mode of transportation – if you're not going by foot, of course – the gondola.

Our gondoliere, a 46-year-old man named Roberto, met us on

the canal outside our hotel, the Bauer Venezia. Roberto has served 26 years in this business and as he paddled us down canal after canal, we got to know a bit about him and his profession:

- Gondolas are individually owned and cost an initial investment of $2,000.
- He wasn't able to tell us how much one could make in a year doing this job but he said it's one of the best gigs you can have!
- There is no set start and end time to a gondeliere's day – they start at sunrise and finish when they please.
- There's apparently only *one* licensed, female-owned and -operated gondola and this gondeliera has not had an easy time getting the respect she deserves.
- Gondolieri must attend one year of training to get their licence. It's a very technical job and requires a lot of skill, never mind needing a solid understanding of water and weather patterns.

It's a bit surreal not to see any vehicles (aside from on Venice's Lido island), and if you're not careful you could easily find yourself a little lost.

Venice is an absolutely wondrous place when you consider how it was built and the history behind it, so if you can, I highly recommend adding it to your list of places to visit *soon*.

And all rules aside, you can choose to kiss under one bridge or over them all!

"You can't blame gravity for
falling in love."
– Albert Einstein

CHAPTER 36

EVEN IF YOU KNOW IT ALL

"Square astronaut, round hole. But somehow,
I'd managed to push myself through it, and here was
the truly amazing part: along the way,
I'd become a good fit. It had only taken 21 years."
– Col. Chris Hadfield

It took me most of a weekend to make my way through the biography of John Wooden, the legendary basketball coach of UCLA, who saw his team through a record winning streak that included 10 championships. The book is long, but a very good, insightful read.

One of the key lessons revolves around what you learn after you know it all. Following are some of the lessons everyone should pay attention to, whether they think they know it all or not.

Never stop learning

Think of yourself as a traveller and always try to look at the world around you with fresh eyes. When we are at home and busy in our day-to-day lives, we get stuck in routines and find it easy to say no to ideas and experiences; however, when we travel, we're much more open to new experiences and because we don't know what to expect, we end up seeing and doing things we never thought we would. Keep that sense of openness and try saying yes more often.

Don't be afraid to get in over your head

Of all the uncomfortable experiences, getting in over your head is probably the one most worth pursuing. Sure, it's a little scary and there's always the chance of failure, but nothing stretches you more or makes you more creative than having no idea what you're doing.

If you want to move up in your career, you must do things that get you noticed. Take on the big challenges and projects no one else wants. It may not always be fun, but you will be better for the effort, and others will see that you are motivated to learn and grow.

Learn to give and take critical feedback

We all want to get better at what we do. In order for that to happen, we must be open to feedback from others. Learning to hear and accept criticism may be one of the most positive things you can do for your career. So instead of taking it personally, think of criticism as a cheat sheet. In giving you direct feedback, your boss, colleague, mentor or coach is offering a shortcut for getting better at the things that will help you be successful.

Sometimes, even when you make a real effort, taking feedback well can be a struggle. Your first impulse may be to get defensive or stop listening: be aware of that. Prepare yourself by taking a breath when you realize criticism is coming your way, then listen to the whole thing without interruption. Write down what you've heard if that helps you process it and ask questions to make sure you're interpreting the feedback correctly.

The flip side of taking feedback is giving it to someone else. Whether you're a manager or a friend, feedback is an opportunity to help someone get better, so don't skip over it, even if it makes you uncomfortable. Good coaches understand the importance of providing direct feedback and doing so in a respectful way. It's important not to try and soften the blow or talk around what it is you need to say. That might make you feel better but it will only confuse the issue and frustrate the other person. If you're struggling to be direct, try framing the issue in one clear sentence followed by some details to back up what you're saying. For example: "Fred, the way you're handling your sales calls isn't working. Let's talk through why . . . "

Feedback is also more constructive and effective when it is accompanied by recent, specific examples. Telling someone they have a bad attitude isn't helpful – it's far better to point to a precise moment when that bad attitude showed up and then explain how moments like that add up and impact others. Ultimately, knowing how to improve is as important as knowing *what* to improve, so the person receiving feedback should leave the conversation feeling empowered to change, not demoralized.

Find a mentor . . . or two . . . or three . . .

If you have heard me speak before or read any of my other books, you know I'm very keen on mentors. That's because I have been blessed in my lifetime to receive support and encouragement from three of the best. My first mentor was Raymond J. Addington, former president of Kelly Douglas. Ray taught me the significance of character and follow-through. My second mentor is Dr. Mel Cooper, owner of CFAX Radio in Victoria. You might also remember him as the vice-president of Expo 86. I first met Mel when I worked at CKNW, and he taught me the importance of a good attitude. Mel once told me, "Your attitude determines your altitude. How high you go is almost entirely due to a positive attitude." My third mentor, as previously mentioned, is Joe Segal, the legendary businessman and philanthropist who showed me the importance of communication, sharing ideas and never giving up.

Nobody is really successful unless other people want them to be. Mentors are people who choose you as much as you choose them. Your responsibility as the recipient of their wisdom is to lead a life that models the qualities that they have nurtured in you.

Always have a goal to work towards

We can't control everything about our lives – interest rates, the economy, the price of housing, the job market – but working towards a goal gives us something positive to focus on and lays the foundation for future success. If you aren't building towards something, you're probably stagnating and when that happens you can start to feel a victim trapped by your own life. The best way to reverse such an unfortunate scenario is to work towards a goal.

No matter what your passion is, get out there and start doing something. As Lao Tzu said, even a journey of a thousand miles begins with a single step.

Today, choose one thing that you've always wanted to do. It might be something from your bucket list, like skydiving or climbing a mountain; or it could be learning a new language or upgrading your education; or perhaps it involves giving back to the community through volunteer work or social activism. Whatever your goal is, put it in writing and then come up with one tangible step you can take right now to set you on your way.

Having a sense of purpose and an exciting goal to work towards makes everything you do feel more meaningful and gives you more control over your life.

Take the first step on a new journey today.

Help others be successful

As success coach Brian Tracy says, "Successful people are

always looking for opportunities to help others. Unsuccessful people are always asking, 'What's in it for me?'" The truth is, our greatest successes in life often come through helping others succeed, and without question, when you focus on helping others succeed your eventual payoff will always be far greater than your investment. This is something I also learned from my mentor Joe Segal, who says, "Alone, you are only as good as your reach, you must join hands with others." According to Joe, joining together with others whose skills complement our own – and who we can depend on to have our back – not only gives us courage, it also allows us to play to our strengths, thereby accomplishing far more than we ever could on our own.

Pass on the knowledge you've acquired

I'm sure you've had a few moments in your career when you've thought to yourself, "I wish someone would have told me about such and such." I know I have. A lot of times, the road to success can feel more like a rollercoaster with all the ups and downs and stomach-churning loops it entails. But now that you have all of this knowledge and life experience under your belt, don't keep it to yourself, put it to work and pass it on.

Develop a positive outlook

Having a positive outlook and surrounding ourselves with optimistic and uplifting people has a direct cause-and-effect on our demeanor, our confidence level and our performance. If you're not always as positive as you'd like to be, there are ways to tune into a more positive outlook. The Mayo Clinic offers five habits that can help you shift into a more positive mode:

- Check yourself for negativity often.
- Be open to humour.
- Strive to live a healthy lifestyle.
- Keep the company of positive people.
- Practise positive self-talk. Start by following one simple rule: Don't say anything to yourself that you wouldn't say to anyone else. Be gentle and encouraging with yourself.

Remember, every day, whether we interact with five people, 50 people or 500, our actions matter and they produce a ripple effect that extends far beyond us. Let's model integrity, celebrate growth, encourage strength and push for positive change.

"People often say that motivation doesn't last.
Well, neither does bathing – that's why we recommend it daily."
– Zig Ziglar

Life's Too Short
In 2005, Steve Jobs delivered a commencement address to the graduating class of Stanford University. Interestingly, Jobs himself was not a college graduate, although that never got in the way of his success. In his address, Jobs focused on the importance of finding a purpose. Here is part of what he had

to say: "Your time is limited, so don't waste it living someone else's life. Don't be trapped by dogma – which is living with the results of other people's thinking. Don't let the noise of other people's opinions drown out your own inner voice. And most important, have the courage to follow your heart and intuition, they somehow already know what you truly want to become. Everything else is secondary."

When my daughters were young, we made a point of introducing them to a variety of foods; this, of course, included vegetables. While we didn't believe in forcing them to eat foods they really didn't like, our philosophy was that they at least had to try what was on their plate.

So it was that we attempted to get our Samantha to eat Brussels sprouts at Sunday dinner. As usual, when dinner was ready, Kay served up a small portion of veggies to each child. Unfortunately for Samantha, when the Brussels sprouts landed on her plate it was not love at first sight. As dinner progressed, she managed to eat around the offending vegetables and, thinking herself finished, asked to be excused.

"No, you may not," Kay said firmly. "You haven't even tried the Brussels sprouts."

"I don't want to try them," said Samantha. "I already know I don't like them."

Not one to give in, Kay held her ground. "When you've finished what's on your plate you may be excused."

After sitting at the table, glaring at the two lonely Brussels sprouts for half an hour, Samantha decided to negotiate (a tactic I would highly recommend to any child in a similar situation).

"If I eat these two Brussels sprouts," she propositioned, "do you promise I'll never have to try them again?"

"Absolutely," Kay agreed. "As long as you try them."

Looking as if a life sentence had been lifted, Samantha quickly ate the vegetables and excused herself.

Years later, in the middle of writing a book, I mentioned to Samantha that I was thinking of including this story in a chapter on priorities.

"Yeah, dad," she said. "That would make a good chapter. After all, life's too short to eat Brussels sprouts."

"Life is too short to wake up in the morning with regrets,
so love the people who treat you right,
forget about the ones who don't and believe that everything
happens for a reason. If you get a chance,
take it. If it changes your life, let it. Nobody said life would
be easy, they just promised it would be worth it."
– Dr. Seuss

CHAPTER 37

YOU CAN *GET* ANYONE IF YOU TRY

"But people could walk the same road
and see different things."
– John Hart

I nfluence is all about building connections; however, we all have people we just don't *get*. Everyone's different and sometimes it's hard to understand those who we perceive to be very different from us. It can also be difficult to open up and accept people we don't feel comfortable around, but the reality is, we don't always get to choose who spends time around us, whether it's a colleague at work, a client or an in-law who's suddenly part of your family. So it makes sense to at least *try* to understand where others are coming from.

According to Dave Kerpen, author of *The Art of People: 11 Simple People Skills That Will Get You Everything You Want,* the first step is to reach out to the person and get to know something about them. "Be interested, rather than interesting," advises Kerpen. "Let them talk about what's important to them."

It's not necessary to like everyone you interact with, but by getting to know a little more about them, at least you can have some empathy and understanding, which will help you develop a more productive relationship. If you have to, consider it an experiment to see if it's possible for you to learn to understand someone very different from you. So go ahead and ask them out for coffee.

Once you're face to face, keep these tips in mind:

- Most of what people think or do isn't about you, it's about them: People don't care about you. This isn't because they are mean, but simply because they're mostly focused on themselves and their concerns, so don't be offended.
- If you haven't been up-front about what you want, need or how you feel, don't get angry when others aren't responding to you the way you want them to. This goes for work relationships as well as personal ones.
- Look for things you have in common rather than differences; people are more likely to remember your similarities and feel a bond when you have common interests.
- People are more likely to help you if there's something in it for them. There are basically four different things that motivate us to help others:

1. **Transactions** – If I buy a car from you, both of us benefit. I get a vehicle, which I want. You get money to improve your lifestyle. This is the predominant form of "selfish altruism" between people who don't have emotional bonds.

2. **Familial** – Blood is thicker than water. We are designed to protect people who share our genes. This sometimes also includes extremely close friends and other loved ones.

3. **Philanthropy** – Helping someone is a sign of status and power. Many species of primates offer assistance as a sign of dominance. People act similarly, offering help to boost their reputation as well as self-esteem. That's what charity is all about.

4. **You owe me one** – Many relationships are based on the idea that if I help you, one day you will help me in return; it's called "implied reciprocity."

- Finally, remember that relationships are a shared responsibility. Don't wait to be invited to gatherings or for others to approach you. Reach out to them and show that you're interested and approachable.

Now for your homework: Write down the names of three people in your life whom you're struggling to connect with. Commit to asking one of them to have coffee with you in the next week, then walk into the coffee meeting determined to *get* this person – even if you find that you still don't like them.

"Be the one who nurtures and builds.
Be the one who has a forgiving heart; one who looks
for the best in people. Leave people better
than you found them."
— Marvin J. Ashton

CHAPTER 38

FIVE WAYS TO INFLUENCE YOUR WELL-BEING

"Energy is the essence of life. Every day
you decide how you're going to use it by knowing
what you want and what it takes to reach
that goal, and by maintaining focus."
– Oprah Winfrey

T he key to happiness may be elusive, but taking advantage of a few simple strategies can do a great deal to improve your everyday feelings of well-being.

1. Let it go
It's important to keep our lives free of unnecessary things. Og Mandino puts it beautifully in the following quote that speaks of our actions as well as the possessions we accumulate.

"Never again clutter your days and nights with so many menial and unimportant things that you have no time to accept a real challenge when it comes along. This applies to play as well as work. A day merely survived is no cause for celebration. You are not here to fritter away your precious hours when you have the ability to accomplish so much by making a slight change in your routine. No more busy work. No more hiding from success. Leave time, leave space, to grow. Now. Now! Not tomorrow!"

Joe Segal once told me, "If you don't need something, rather than hold onto it, give it to someone who does." For many of us, it's easy to say but hard to do, just ask anyone who's tried to "KonMari" their life after watching *Tidying Up* on Netflix. It's amazing how attached we become to all of "our stuff," as the late comedian George Carlin was famous for joking about. The scary part is that for many people it is really getting out of control.

> Clearing out the stuff in your life that you no longer use doesn't just get rid of old junk that's getting in your way; it also frees up your mind and creates room for you to move forward with important plans.

Maclean's magazine did a story on North America's fastest-growing real estate segment, the storage business, which generates $22 billion per year in revenue. In fact, in the span of just one decade, the amount of this kind of storage in the United States has more than doubled to an area larger than Manhattan and San Francisco combined.

Interestingly, the article noted that many of the people who rent these storage lockers have a greater volume of "stuff" in storage than they have in their own homes and they are paying money to keep it there because they don't have room for it anywhere else – because of all their other "stuff." Imagine how much easier their lives would be if they just ditched some of it.

So, here's the question you knew was coming, "What part of your life needs tidying up?" Is it your basement, your car, your desk at work, your computer hard drive, that drawer or closet where you put everything that doesn't have a place? Maybe it's all of these.

Clearing out the stuff you no longer use doesn't just get rid of old junk that's getting in your way; it also frees up your mind and creates room for you to move forward with important plans and goals. So don't store your stuff, make a decision on what can stay and what needs to go.

When you've rid your life of unnecessary clutter, suddenly you'll have a much clearer view of everything valuable that you do have and feel infinitely more productive, with more room to think and breathe.

2. Just breathe

Belongings aren't the only things we hold onto unnecessarily. Holding onto anything, according to Deepak Chopra, whether it is an event in the past or a preconceived idea of what the future should be, is like holding your breath. Ultimately, you'll suffocate. Letting go of things and learning to live in the present moment can be extremely difficult (I know it is for me), but mindfulness, as it is often called, can be as simple as breathing. Seriously, one of the simplest ways to experience "living in the moment" can be done as you go about your daily activities, and it all stems from focusing on your breathing.

Here's a simple exercise to try. It involves breathing from your belly, not your chest.

First, sit or stand in a relaxed position. Now, slowly inhale through our nose until you feel that you can't take in any more air. As you prepare to slowly exhale, firm up your belly and tighten your abdominal muscles to push the air up and out of your lungs. Repeat this process several times.

Here are a few more tips:

1. As you breathe, let your abdomen expand outward rather than raising your shoulders. This is a more relaxed and natural way to breathe. It also helps your lungs fill more fully with fresh air and push out more old air.

2. Try a few breaths any time you want to release tension, or for several minutes as a form of meditation.

3. If you like, make your throat a little tighter as you exhale so the air comes out like an exaggerated sigh. This type of breathing is used in yoga and can bring additional relaxation.

Mindfulness is an acquired skill. Its stress-reduction benefits are well-documented and there are many positive emotional and spiritual side effects as well. As your skill at mindfulness increases, you will, by definition, let go of things in the past or worries about the future.

Take some time to practise mindfulness and consciously breathe every day.

3. Take a hike or try a little forest-bathing

A recent article by *Conde Nast Traveler* talks about how hiking can actually change our brain. "From lessening negativity to boosting creativity, hiking in fresh air actually boosts brain power and can help certain parts of the brain grow," writes Meredith Carey, who outlines three brain benefits.

The first is our ability to problem solve. Being in the outdoors and away from the distractions of technology can raise cognitive function by as much as 50 per cent, resulting in better problem solving and more creative thinking.

The second benefit is related to memory. Studies show that walking in nature impacts the hippocampus, which is the brain's memory hub and can help stave off Alzheimer's and other memory-related illnesses. Some countries in Europe have gone so far as to recommend citizens get a minimum dose of five hours of nature per month to improve mental health and memory.

Finally, hiking helps cut down on negativity. Studies at Stanford University found that walking in nature helps to reduce blood flow in the subgenual prefrontal cortex (the area of the brain associated with negative thinking) and eliminate the obsessive and negative thoughts we all experience from time to time, particularly when we are brooding about something. So not only does a walk or hike provide you with physical exercise, it benefits your brain and your mood.

Even if hiking isn't your thing, you might want to spend some time in the forest to boost your immune system. The practice of forest-bathing or Shinrin-yoku was introduced in the 1980s in Japan and has recently become popular in the West. Forest-bathing, which could be described as a walking meditation through the forest, is an opportunity to savour the sounds, smells and sights of nature, without any particular goal or destination in mind.

4. Accept your emotions

"Some would argue that most of our physical, mental and relational problems come from our inability to adequately experience emotions," according to clinical psychologist Ryan Howes. "We deny, bury, project, rationalize, medicate, drink away, smother in comfort food, sleep off, sweat out, suck [it] up and sweep under the rug our sadness, anger and fear."

Some people spend more energy avoiding their emotions than others do on actually feeling them, he said. So the key is to give yourself permission to feel your feelings. Per Howes: "When you feel safe enough to let your guard down, whether that's alone or with someone you trust, you can focus on the situation, fully experience the feelings and begin to better understand why it hurts and what you want to do about the situation."

Writing about negative emotions can also help to process feelings that may seem overwhelming. People who write about their deepest emotions feel less depressed and more positive about life.

5. Take a nap, it's good for you

A feature story in *Chatelaine*'s March 2016 magazine caught my attention with the headline: "Doze Your Way to Success."

Studies have shown people who take a daily nap have lower blood pressure and an increased tolerance for frustration.

Kimberly Cote, a psychology professor and director of Brock University's sleep research lab, says napping is proven to boost alertness, mood and memory. There are other benefits as well; research conducted by the European Society of Cardiology found that people who took a daily nap had lower blood pressure, and the University of Michigan linked napping at work to increased tolerance for frustration, higher productivity and less impulsive behaviour.

Dr. Cote recommends taking a 20-minute power nap in the afternoon when you can, which is just long enough to reap the benefits of rest without getting into the deep stages of sleep.

Some people might equate napping with being lazy, but being lazy isn't necessarily bad, according to Bill Gates, who says: "I choose a lazy person to do a hard job, because a lazy person will find an easy way to do it."

Although he didn't like to talk about it, Thomas Edison was a habitual napper, which was probably the secret to his remarkable productivity. Once, when Henry Ford stopped by Edison's lab for a visit, Edison's assistant stopped him from entering the office because Edison was taking a nap. When Ford looked confused and said, "But I thought Edison didn't sleep very much," the assistant replied, "He doesn't sleep very much at all, he just naps a lot."

A form of micro-napping practised by the likes of Einstein, Aristotle and surrealist artist Salvador Dali, has more recently gained scientific credence for its usefulness in sparking creative ideas and problem solving. Known as a hypnogogic nap, the way Dali did it was to fall asleep sitting in a chair with a key in his hand and a pie plate on the floor directly below the hand with the key. As he dozed off, his hand would relax. When his hand relaxed enough to drop the key, the clank of the key on the pie plate would wake him and he would immediately jump to his canvas to create based on the ideas that came to him in that hypnogogic state between dreaming and wakefulness. Einstein described using a similar technique to sharpen his problem-solving abilities during the day. The trick with micro-napping is to wake yourself before you get to stage-two sleep, after which it is much harder to regain full alertness.

"I like a lot of things about yoga – it's an intro to good music;
with each good teacher you study with, you learn
a lot about them personally; it's not just about specific
technique or poses. I also like Shavasana – not too many
exercise routines let you nap at the end of them. You don't see
nap pods in CrossFit gyms."
– Charles Michael Davis

CHAPTER 39

DR. NIDO QUBEIN

"Without continual growth and progress,
such words as improvement, achievement and success
have no meaning."
– Benjamin Franklin

D r. Nido Qubein is a legend in the professional speaking world and a longtime member of the Speakers Roundtable. As mentioned earlier, the roundtable is limited to just 20 professional speakers based in North America. Members don't apply, they're invited, and I was lucky enough to receive a phone call one Sunday evening nearly two decades ago from Brian Tracy asking if I would like to join. I later learned that I am the only Canadian who has ever been asked, so I consider it a rare and special privilege.

I suspect that Nido had something to do with my nomination.

Over the 20 years that I have been a Speakers Roundtable member, Nido and I have become even closer and his influence on my life has been considerable.

He is a consummate professional in all that he does. In 2005, he was asked to be the president of High Point University in North Carolina. You could say that High Point is a sleepy little town, but Nido's transformation of this world-class university has been nothing short of amazing and he is committed to helping students develop themselves. "Teaching people skills without giving them a vision for a better future is only training," he explains. "A leader inspires and grows people. If I don't grow people, there will be no future for this institution."

"For many people, change is more threatening than it is challenging," says Nido. "They see it as the destroyer of what is familiar and comfortable rather than the creator of what is new and exciting."

His motto for the students is, "I'm focused on planting seeds of greatness in the minds, hearts and souls of all those I'm blessed to encounter."

While he encourages students to dream big, Nido also believes you must be practical and consistent to achieve your dreams. "If the first time you fail you give up, you'll never do anything in life," he explains. "You have to be consistently focused on executing important things in life to make them happen."

Nido also reminds his students that, "Success doesn't come

to you; you must go to it. The trail is well-travelled. If you walk it, you can get there."

Nido encourages his students to set themselves up for success through the habits they create. "Most of our choices emerge from our habitual process," he says. "Choices become habits and determine what you do with your life. The irony about habits is that bad habits are easy to develop and hard to live with."

When it comes to success, Nido reminds us that the real competition isn't with others: "Winners compare their achievements with their goals, while losers compare their achievements with those of other people." And setting goals that are personally meaningful is the best way to ensure success. "When a goal matters enough to a person, that person will find a way to accomplish what at first seemed impossible."

Nido himself is no stranger to the challenges of life. After losing his father when he was just six years old, Nido was raised by his mother and arrived in the United States (from his home country of Jordan) in 1966 as a teenager with little knowledge of English and only $50 in his pocket. Determined to speak fluently, he practised English every day using three-by-five index cards and has since gone on to write 18 books in a language that was not his native tongue.

"For many people, change is more threatening than it is challenging," says Nido. "They see it as the destroyer of what is familiar and comfortable rather than the creator of what is new and exciting."

For Nido, America was filled with opportunity and he couldn't wait to start building his future.

"With every venture, I learned new things," he says. "With every risk I took, I matured and evolved."

After building a distinguished career as a business leader, Nido was invited to become president of High Point University in 2005. In the 14 years since, his commitment to the university that he attended as a young man has helped to transform High Point into a world-class educational institution. "A decision is made with the brain while a commitment is made with the heart," says Nido. "Therefore, a commitment is much deeper and more binding than a decision."

For years, as president of High Point, Nido has emphasized the transformative nature of cultivating a growth mindset to his student audiences, because he believes it will change their understanding of what it means to learn. Since 2016, Nido and his faculty team have been on a journey to infuse growth mindset techniques into every aspect of campus life, encouraging students to stretch themselves intellectually.

"Individuals with a growth mindset are better prepared for the world not just as it is, but as it's going to be in the future," explains Nido. "They're knowledge seekers. They work hard, they fail, they learn from their mistakes, and thus, they grow."

As someone who has achieved great things, Nido has some helpful advice for anyone who is feeling stuck: "One of the greatest reasons people cannot mobilize themselves is that they try to accomplish great things. Most worthwhile achievements are the result of many little things done in a single direction; break down your objectives into small steps and implement those steps one by one to move forward."

"Spectacular achievement is always preceded
by unspectacular preparation."
– Robert H. Schuller

CHAPTER 40

KNOW WHERE TO PUT YOUR FOCUS

"I don't care how much power, brilliance or energy
you have, if you don't harness it and focus
it on a specific target and hold it there, you're never going
to accomplish as much as your ability warrants."
– Zig Ziglar

L ast summer, I had the chance to study for one week at Oxford University on "Christian Leadership."

When I shared news of the opportunity with my wife Kay, she said, "By all means Peter, *go*, but no cutting classes!"

Kay knows me all too well . . . in a place like Oxford, it would be difficult not to wander off and get distracted.

True to my word, I didn't cut class. My days started at 8 a.m. and the formal program ended at 6 p.m. each day.

This was a once in a lifetime kind of thing.

While I was at Oxford, we stayed in the (very tiny) dorm rooms at Magdalen College, one of the most revered colleges at Oxford.

On graduation day, we gathered in the main hall and I looked up at the paintings of scholars all around the room. One in particular caught my eye and upon asking, I learned that it was a portrait of Cardinal Wolsey – chief aide to Henry VIII.

I also discovered that Roger Bannister had been a student of the college.

Now, if you don't know his name, Roger Bannister was the first runner to break the "four-minute mile."

Bannister trained at Magdalen College, partly due to the measurements on the quadrangle behind the school. It was exactly one mile in distance. As a young medical student, he calculated that he needed to run 5,280 steps in 240 seconds and his gait would need to be enough to cover 22 inches with every stride. Bannister embarked on a rigorous exercise program to increase his lung capacity and achieve the exact stride needed. The path around Magdalen provided the perfect training ground for him.

> Whether you are running a race or running a business, it's easy to get distracted. That's why it's imperative you know where to put your focus in order to achieve your goals.

On March 6, 1954, Bannister broke the four-minute mile, completing the distance in 3:59:04.

Later that year, a chap named John Landy from Australia

also broke the four-minute mile.

In August of 1954, the British Empire Games were scheduled to be held right here in Vancouver at Empire Stadium (you probably know it as the site of the PNE). Both Bannister and Landy were entered in the race along with several other runners from around the world – but all eyes were on these two.

The race would be the highlight of the Games and afterward it was written into history as "The Miracle Mile."

My father Bernie was in the stands that day and the crowd was enormous.

The eight runners lined up.

The starter's gun went off and the race was on.

Four times around the track.

On the final lap, Landy the Australian was in the lead with Bannister only 7-10 yards behind him. Just before the finish line, Landy looked back over his left shoulder (rather than his right) and as he looked the wrong way, Bannister shot right past him and won the race.

Bannister had once again broken the four-minute mile with a time of 3:57:04 but that wasn't the real story here. The real story was that Landy looked the wrong way . . . and completely missed his opportunity to be the man in the record books.

The city commemorated that fateful race with a bronze statue of John Landy looking back over the wrong shoulder. It still stands outside the PNE grounds adjacent to where Empire Stadium once stood.

Whether you are running a race or running a business, it's easy to get distracted. That's why it's imperative you know where to put your focus in order to achieve your goals.

> *"The main thing is that you keep the main thing,*
> *the main thing."*
> – Stephen Covey

When it comes to growing your business or your career, there will always be a multitude of areas competing for your attention – and most of them will seem important – but the reality is that there are only a handful of things you can and should focus on at one time. That's where strategic priorities come in.

Having too many "important" things to do at once is distracting and it dilutes the effectiveness of your efforts.

How to Determine Your Strategic Priorities

Here are a few tips for helping figure out what you should be focusing on based on an article by leadership expert Stephanie Pollock.

As a business leader, planning is essential to your success and no doubt you set goals and objectives for yourself and/ or your business each year. If you don't have one already, sit down and make a list of your top business or career priorities for the year ahead (you don't have to wait for January 1 to do this exercise, you can do it anytime).

From your list, pick at least three, but not more than five priorities that are the most important areas for the growth and success of you and your business. These are your strategic priorities. Once you've identified your priorities, you essentially have your areas of focus and that's where you need to put all of your effort until you've achieved these goals. By focusing your efforts, not only are you saying "yes" to what you want to achieve (and setting yourself up for success), you're also giving yourself permission to say "no" or "not right now" to anything that isn't directly related to one of your priorities.

So let's say you've identified three strategic priorities:

- Build a solid list to prepare for the launch of your online marketing program.
- Create a stable base of consulting clients.
- Sell at least 500 subscriptions for your marketing program.

Now, let's say you get an email from one of your favourite marketing influencers promoting their podcast course. You say to yourself, "Maybe I should learn how to do a podcast to promote my marketing program. It seems to be the latest thing and I don't want to miss out."

Tell me this isn't the kind of thing that sidetracks you from focusing on your priorities . . . it happens to all of us, but before you jump in, look at the priorities you identified. Can you see a direct relationship between learning how to do a podcast and any of your priorities? I can't.

Sure, you could talk yourself into it. You could argue that you might be able to get some people from the podcast to join your email list. You *might* even land a few new consulting clients based on your great insights, but it's not a direct line. Although a podcast might be cool and fun to do, it's most likely not going to produce the results you need.

Now, let's take another example. Say you're invited to speak at a conference that caters to small business owners (the kind of clients who would love your marketing program). Since you haven't included public speaking as a strategic priority, you're wondering if it's a fit. The answer is yes. Speaking is a fantastic way to get new clients and you could definitely leverage the opportunity to have sales conversations with attendees. What's more, you could offer a special incentive for them to join your email list. You could also focus your talk specifically on content that would support your marketing program, prepping them to take the next step with you. You could effectively support all three of your strategic priorities with one speech and then leverage that speech into content for your blog or a few social media posts.

So you say "no" to podcasting and "yes" to the speech; that's how you decide where to focus your attention.

The acid test: if it doesn't support your strategic priorities, you don't do it, full stop!

Remember to keep your strategic priorities front and centre on a day-to-day basis so you can make sure you're hitting them when you set up your calendar. You don't need to work on all three every day, but you do need to make sure they are all getting enough attention.

> *"The key is not to prioritize what's on your schedule,*
> *but to schedule your priorities."*
> – Stephen Covey

CHAPTER 41

IAN TELFER – THE MAN WITH THE GOLD SHOES

"Life is either a daring adventure or nothing at all."
– Helen Keller

W hen I first met Ian Telfer, the man behind Goldcorp Inc., one of Vancouver's biggest success stories, he said something that I've not stopped thinking about since: "If you're not in the storm, you will never get hit by lightning. There is no reward without risk."

He was right on.

If you're not putting yourself out there, if you're not asking for the sale, if you're not taking a chance, you will *never* get lucky.

Well, this wasn't the only gem he had for me. In 2018, I interviewed Ian at the *BCBusiness* Top 100 event, where he walked onstage wearing a pair of shiny gold running shoes.

Ian has a fantastic sense of humour and is full of insight and wisdom from a life lived to the fullest, of taking risks and going off gut-feelings. And it's paid off! In early 2019, Newmont Mining Corp. agreed to acquire Goldcorp for $10 billion, creating the world's largest gold company.

Ian may be known for his business success and for turning a struggling company into one of the world's most successful gold mining entities, but equally impressive is his philanthropic work and commitment to bettering the lives of people who live in the towns and villages he mines out of.

Giving back to the community comes naturally to Ian and he sees it as his responsibility to leave every community even better than when they first broke ground. In the past two years, Ian has been celebrated by Variety – The Children's Charity and the Fraser Institute as well as being inducted into the Canadian Business Hall of Fame. Another organization that is close to his heart is Junior Achievement, which partners with business and community leaders to provide financial literacy and entrepreneurship training to young people.

> If you're not putting yourself out there, if you're not asking for the sale, if you're not taking a chance, you will *never* get lucky.

Ian is also a great champion of higher education. In 2007, he donated $25 million to the University of Ottawa's business school, which was later renamed the Telfer School of Management; he also established a scholarship at the Telfer School, which is awarded annually to the MBA student accepted with the lowest grade marks.

The gold mining industry, which fluctuates wildly between bull markets and bear markets and back again, is not for the faint of heart. After more than 30 years as a business leader, Telfer knows a thing or two about seizing opportunity and he offers this advice:

"First of all, don't let fear of failure stop you from taking advantage of a potential opportunity. In the mining industry, most companies spend years looking for gold, they don't give up . . . they believe in something that others can't see.

"Secondly, I think a lot of entrepreneurs believe that when opportunity arrives, it presents itself with a big bang and is clear as day. I'm sure that's the case sometimes. But, more often than not, opportunity comes in quietly and you have to be really attuned to your surroundings (and the business environment) to be the first one to hear it. When you see an opportunity, be bold and seize it!

"One other point that I wish I knew when I was starting out and a point I reiterate to students and the younger generation of professionals is to be the business partner you wish you had. Putting yourself in another person's shoes is never the easiest thing to do, but it's incredibly worthwhile when building business relationships or building a business with a partner.

"Commit to being a partner who brings unique tools and skill sets to the table. By the same token, choose partners who have skills that complement, rather than compete, with your own.

And look for associates who can challenge your way of thinking and offer fresh perspective and insight.

"Finally, I think being a business leader means learning from one's mistakes. And that's OK. We have to be free to fail, in business and in life too. Hopefully, these words of guidance can provide a little measure of help along the way."

"If you dare nothing, then when the day is over,
nothing is all you will have gained."
– Neil Gaiman

CHAPTER 42

THE FORTUNATE ONES

*"In ordinary life we hardly realize that we
receive a great deal more than we give and that it is
only with gratitude that life becomes rich."*
– Dietrich Bonhoeffer

W e live in a country where the majority of people are what I would call over-privileged. Logically, you'd think that would make us endlessly thankful for what we have – especially if we happen to pay attention to what is going on in the rest of the world. But more often than not, we feel entitled to even more.

Whenever I speak to an audience about how much abundance we have in our lives, I always say that we can all come up with at least 15 things to be grateful for. When we are verbally grateful for the blessings in our life, it changes everything: our perspective on how much we need, our sense of entitlement . . . and most importantly, our attitude – which has a direct influence on our overall happiness. I don't know about you, but I would rather be happy. If you would too, consider the following:

- If you woke up this morning with more health than illness, you are more blessed than the millions who will not survive this week.
- If you have never experienced the danger of battle, the loneliness of imprisonment, the agony of torture or the pangs of starvation, you are more fortunate than 500 million people in the world.
- If you can attend a religious meeting without fear of harassment, arrest, torture or death, you are more blessed than three billion people in the world.
- If you have enough food to eat, clothes on your back, a roof overhead and a place to sleep, you are richer than 75 per cent of this world.

> Never forget that you are one of the fortunate ones. Count your blessings every day and soon you too will realize just how privileged you truly are.

- If you have money in the bank, in your wallet and spare change in a dish someplace, you are among the top eight per cent of the world's wealthy.
- If you hold up your head with a smile on your face and are

truly thankful, you are blessed because the majority can, but most choose not to.

- If you can hold someone's hand, hug them or even pat them on the shoulder, you are blessed because you can offer a healing touch.
- Never forget that you are one of the fortunate ones. Count your blessings every day and soon you too will realize just how privileged you truly are.

"Piglet noticed that even though he
had a very small heart, it could hold a
rather large amount of gratitude."
– A.A. Milne

CHAPTER 43

THE BACK NINE

"If you think it's hard to meet new people,
try picking up the wrong golf ball."
– Jack Lemmon

My wife and I are avid golfers – we're not very good – but sometimes we break 100 and feel very proud of ourselves. I expect on average, between the Vancouver Golf Club and spending some time at our place in Palm Springs, we play about 60-70 times per year.

As with many of our friends and associates, we are in the back nine of our lives. Thankfully, we are both in pretty good health and happily married for more than five decades; however, we realize there are more years behind us than there are in front of us.

My former business partner of over 20 years, who is still a very good friend, Neil Soper, forwarded me this piece called "The

Back Nine – and Then It Is Winter," which I have included below. I close this book encouraging you to end well, live well, be happy, and stay married and in love for life.

The Back Nine – and Then It Is Winter

You know . . . time has a way of moving quickly and catching you unaware of the passing years. It seems just yesterday that I was young, just married and embarking on my new life with my mate. Yet in a way, it seems like eons ago and I wonder where all the years went. I know that I lived them all. I have glimpses of how it was back then and of all my hopes and dreams. But, here it is . . . the "back nine" of my life and it catches me by surprise . . . How did I get here so fast? Where did the years go and where did my youth go?

I remember well seeing older people through the years and thinking that those older people were years away from me and that I was only on the first hole and the back nine was so far off that I could not fathom it or imagine fully what it would be like.

But, here it is . . . my friends are retired and getting grey . . .

> I close this book encouraging you to end well, live well, be happy, and stay married and in love for life.

they move slower and I see an older person now. Some are better and some worse . . . but, I see the great change . . . Not like the ones that I remember who were young and vibrant . . . but, like me, their age is beginning to show and we are now those older folks that we used to see and never thought we'd become.

Each day now, I find that just getting a shower is a real target for the day! And taking a nap is not a treat anymore ... It's mandatory! 'Cause if I don't on my own free will ... I just fall asleep where I sit! And so now I enter into this new season of my life unprepared for all the aches and pains and the loss of strength and ability to go and do things that I wish I had done but never did! But, at least I know, that though I'm on the back nine, and I'm not sure how long it will last . . . this I know, that when it's over on this earth . . . it's over. A new adventure will begin! Yes, I have regrets. There are things I wish I hadn't done . . . things I should have done, but indeed, there are many things I'm happy to have done. It's all in a lifetime.

So, if you're not on the "back nine" yet . . . let me remind you, that it will be here faster than you think. So, whatever you would like to accomplish in your life, please do it quickly! Don't put things off too long! Life goes by quickly. So, do what you can today, as you can never be sure whether you're on the "back nine" or not!

You have no promise that you will see all the seasons of your life . . . so, live for today and say all the things that you want your loved ones to remember . . . and hope that they appreciate and love you for all the things that you have done for them in all the years past.

Life is a gift to you. The way you live your life is your gift to those who come after. Make it a fantastic one. LIVE IT WELL!

ENJOY TODAY! DO SOMETHING FUN! BE HAPPY! HAVE A GREAT DAY! Remember, it is health that is real wealth and not pieces of gold and silver.

LASTLY, CONSIDER THIS:

- Your kids are becoming you . . . but your grandchildren are perfect!
- Going out is good . . . Coming home is better!
- You forget names . . . but it's OK because other people forgot they even knew you.
- You realize you're never going to be really good at anything, especially golf.
- The things you used to care to do, you no longer care to do, but you really do care that you don't care to do them anymore.
- You sleep better on a lounge chair with the TV blaring than in bed. It's called "pre-sleep."
- You miss the days when everything worked with just an "ON" and "OFF" switch.
- You tend to use more four-letter words . . . "what?" . . . "when?" . . ."
- Now that you can afford expensive jewelry, it's not safe to wear it anywhere.
- You notice everything they sell in stores is "sleeveless"?!
- What used to be freckles are now liver spots.
- Everybody whispers.

- You have three sizes of clothes in your closet . . . two of which you will never wear.
- But Old is good in some things: old songs, old movies and best of all, OLD FRIENDS!

Stay well, "OLD FRIEND!" Send this on to other "Old Friends" and let them laugh in AGREEMENT!

It's not what you gather, but what you scatter that tells what kind of life you have lived.

Today is the oldest you've ever been, it's also the youngest you'll ever be, so enjoy this day while it lasts.

About the Author

Dr. Peter Legge, O.B.C. • L.L.D. (HON.) • CSP • CPAE • HOF

Peter Legge is chairman and CEO of Canada Wide Media Limited, the largest independently owned publishing company in Western Canada, controlling a network of magazines with multimillions in sales annually.

In addition, Peter travels the world as a motivational speaker, accepting more than 100 assignments each year from clients who know that when he speaks, his words will be a catalyst for positive change. He has received the prestigious Golden Gavel Award from Toastmasters International and was voted "Top Speaker in North America," in company with Dr. Robert Schuller and Stephen Covey. Peter has also been inducted into the Speakers Hall of Fame by both the National Speakers Association in the United States and the Canadian Association of Professional Speakers.

Peter is tireless in his commitment to many worthwhile organizations. As co-host of the annual Variety — The Children's Charity Telethon for over 40 years, he assisted in raising more than $200 million for the charity. He is also an International Ambassador for Variety International.

His efforts have not gone unnoticed. Among his many honours, Peter has received the Golden Heart Award from The Variety Club and has been invested into the Venerable Order of St. John of Jerusalem, where he was subsequently promoted to Commander.

He has been awarded the Order of the Red Cross and named

Citizen of the Year for his commitment to the community.

He has been presented with four honorary doctorate degrees from Simon Fraser University, Royal Roads University, British Columbia Institute of Technology and Douglas College.

He is also a past chair of the Vancouver Board of Trade, and a recipient of the Nido Qubein Philanthropy Award, presented to him at the National Speakers Association Convention in Atlanta in July 2005.

In 2006, he was appointed one of 18 ambassadors to the Vancouver 2010 Olympic and Paralympic Winter Games. In the same year, Sales and Marketing Executives International awarded Peter with the Ambassador of Free Enterprise in Dallas, Texas.

In 2008, he was presented with the Province of British Columbia's highest honour, The Order of British Columbia.

Peter is the author of over 20 books that have inspired thousands of readers the world over with their powerful motivating messages. In all that he has achieved, Peter attributes his success to four factors: persistence, patience, a positive attitude and passion.

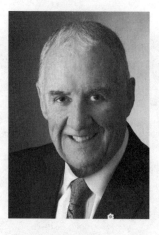

You can contact Dr. Peter Legge, OBC at:
Peter Legge Management Company Ltd.
#230 - 4321 Still Creek Drive
Burnaby, B.C. V5C 6S7 Canada
Telephone: 604.473.0332
Email: *plegge@canadawide.com*
Website: *peterlegge.com*

Follow Peter
LinkedIn.com/in/peterblegge
Twitter: @_peterlegge
Facebook: Insights by Peter Legge OBC
Instagram: insightsofaceo
YouTube: Peter Legge